Day Trading in th...
2020-2030
From Zero to Pa...

Practical Guide for Newbies to Learn How ... *Forex,*
Cryptocurrency, Stocks, Options, ... *in 11 Easy Steps*

Dexter Wade & Flavio Simeri

THE MINDSET OF
THE TRUE TRADER

Let's begin by dealing with Money Management, Risk Management and Portfolio Management: in short, all those aspects which are extremely underrated but at the same time are the most important concerning the Trading of cryptocurrencies and not.

Obviously, we will exemplify and contextualize everything by making reference to the Bitcoin and the cryptocurrencies.

In particular, here is what we are going to analyze step by step:

- The first chapter will be dedicated to the basic concepts;
- The second chapter will be dedicated to the applied operation;
- The third chapter will be dedicated to the self-evaluation of one's own strategies, aimed at the constant improvement of these in order to adapt to the market (that is extremely changeable in the case of the cryptos) and in order to never lose focus on what we are doing.

So, let's get started....

The chapters will be very simple, understandable and suitable for everyone, because we will start from scratch together and I will accompany you on this path. We will get rid of all the wrong preconceptions about Trading and of all the nonsense we read around.

We will set the correct mindset trying to understand what our goals can be and where we could arrive, keeping our feet on the ground and making some paradigm shifts, which many do not do.

If we succeed to do this, we will place ourselves in front of the great majority of "Traders" (between inverted commas because many improvise as such...). At the end of this chapter, I would like you to know:

- What the objectives to keep in mind are;
- What you must concentrate on;
- What you need to get rid of.

These are the foundations on which we will build a trading strategy that should be profitable in the long run, and not just while we are lucky.

Now let's introduce the world of trading, specifically crypto trading.

Let's try to understand which concepts regarding Trading we should forget and which ones we should keep in mind instead. Let's see how to approach this world without illusions, with our feet on the ground and with extreme concreteness, in order to set the correct mindset.

This seems obvious and banal, but in reality, it is the basis of everything.

We should start our path from zero, build the foundations a little at a time and then operate on them.

In fact, operation without the conceptual foundations means nothing.

So, let's start from here.

LET'S DISPEL SOME MYTHS ABOUT TRADING

Let's start with the myths about Trading which should be debunked and then let's try to understand which concepts are useful to free our mind from the wrong ones, namely that:

"Trading allows you to earn a lot in a short time".

I'm sure you have already heard this sentence many times. This is a myth as big as a house because, especially if you start from scratch, it would be fair to say that Trading allows you to lose so much in a short time if you have no method.

So, let's delete this idea from our mind and understand the fact that Trading is a long path that involves self-discovery and has a lot to do with the psychological aspect (you will find out over time).

Above all, it should be pointed out that it is a growth path and therefore it is long by definition.

"You can earn in a constant way over time".

Nothing more wrong here too, because, as we will see shortly, Trading is a game of probability and as such there is the probability of gaining or losing in every position you open and close.

Therefore, consistency is impossible to achieve.

It is possible to reach a condition where your capital grows over time.

But you cannot say: "Every month I make 2%!" or "Every month I make 5%!". This is nonsense. Running after such figures implies certain failure because we really miss the target.

"Just learn to read charts to become profitable!"

Again, nothing could be more wrong, because reading the charts is important, but it represents only one brick and perhaps among other things it is one of the bricks to be placed higher, because at the base there is the correct capital and risk management that is precisely the objective of this path.

So, reading the charts is the last thing to learn, because then there is everything else that must allow us not to disintegrate our capital, opening positions incorrectly.

"Just copy someone else's strategy, positions and signals!"

More nonsense!

5

Why?

Because strategies are extremely personal. We will see this shortly and we will talk about the fact that there is a very strong psychological component that takes into account our character, which is unique and therefore we must adopt a strategy that goes well with our character and our emotionality.

We can then take inspiration from other people's positions and strategies to improve and learn (this is a very good thing that I encourage you to do), but to copy what someone else does is a big mistake because we will never have the same performance, because we are two different people.

The last myth (actually, it's not the last one, but it's the last one that came to my mind!):

"I can finally quit my job and become a Trader in no time!"

This is unfortunately another commonplace typical of the internet, which describes the figure of the Trader always on the beach, in nice cars and so on, but in reality, this is a purely commercial figure and aimed at marketing.

Trust me, you won't leave your job in a matter of.... not even years!

First, there is a long path of learning how to build capital and a strategy and maybe in the future you may have the goal of devoting more to Trading rather than investing and, in part or even entirely, leaving your job (but if you keep on reading, you will understand that it is really a long, long, long path).

So, forget about the fact that in three months you will work as a Trader from morning to night, because this concept is very far from reality.

NUMBERS AND STATISTICS

Let's look at some facts, numbers and statistics instead:

90% of "Traders" are not profitable because they lack consistency.

I have written the word "Traders" in inverted commas precisely because, in reality, in my opinion, they cannot even be defined as Traders, because they are those who do not succeed in constructing a strategy, they do not succeed in being consistent.

Perhaps they read an announcement, an advertisement of some Broker that made them believe that it is easy to make Trading, also with little capital, and earn immediately...

One tries and loses!

And I believe that the majority of that 90% of unprofitable ones recognize themselves in all that.

Others think that the only important thing is the single position, that is to take the opportunity at the right time, to buy and exit and immediately become rich.

In reality, this is not the case at all!

Unfortunately, there are a lot of preconceptions of this kind, such as: "If you had bought that years ago..." "If you had bought Bitcoins in 2009 you would be rich now!".

Yes, but you shouldn't think like that: this is not trading, this is gambling and it's a very different thing.

It's nothing but a gamble.

It's easy to make such reasoning in retrospect, but then you find out that a lot of people who got into Bitcoin in 2017 are not rich at all now, in fact they may have lost a lot of their capital and be at a net loss.

100% of those who praise their profits on Facebook or on the web are impostors.

We should never take anything for granted because, especially on the web, on Facebook or on other social networking sites, 100% (here I'm sure) of those who slam their profits in your face saying "Look how good we are! We've made +80%, +90%!" are certainly talking about profits in percentages, without capital at risk, without data on the capital used, on Risk Management and so on. This makes us immediately understand that they are just impostors who probably want to sell us some course or monthly subscription to their phantom Premium groups and stuff like that.

So, I urge you to stay away from this scum!

Purpose: Long-term profitability.

That's what trading is all about: setting up a strategy that works over the long term (long term means years).

It means that the curve of your overall capital must grow over time, which means that your strategies are working.

You can also suffer losses, one after the other, but be profitable in the long run.

That's what trading is all about: sometimes you gain, sometimes you lose.

It is essential to shift the focus from the single position to the strategy as a whole.

If our gains outweigh our losses, it means that we are profitable.

If, on the other hand, it's the losses that exceed the gains, we must modify something.

To do this, it is essential to shift the focus from the single position to the strategy as a whole, so from gamblers/bettors we become traders.

Gambling means focusing 100% on the single position to the extreme and go all-in on something.

When you hear people say "I only bought this one and I'm keeping it there because I want to open a position only on that", that's crazy!

We can do it cumulatively: for example, if we want to make a long-term investment but we are not talking about trading, if we use all our capital for a single position, that is beyond any logic.

If we do not diversify and mitigate risk, we are making a huge mistake.

The main objective of the strategy must be to minimize risk and safeguard capital.

Also here we should make a so-called "paradigm shift", that is to shift the focus from the objective we usually have (the gain) to the opposite, that is to minimize the losses and to safeguard the capital.

The gain comes naturally, but the main objective must be to protect the capital.

You realize this especially when it starts to grow.

IS IT ALL A GAME OF PROBABILITY?

In Trading, each position has a probability associated with itself, which is difficult to quantify.

By looking at things more from above, it is easier to make some quantifications.

By putting several positions together over a longer period of time and categorizing them in a certain way, it is easier to make some statistics.

This is a better way to operate than focusing on the single position.

There is no such thing as a position to which a certain result can be attributed.

What do I mean? I mean that if it's making a bullish right triangle pattern, it doesn't necessarily mean that it's really bullish!

It can also be bearish.

If the RSI is oversold, it is not certain that the price will go up, it can easily go down again.

The future cannot be predicted.

That's it: there are no certain results. You must not think that you can predict the future by reading the chart.

This is not what you should do with the technical analysis and the chart analysis.

We will deal with this point better below here.

Few things are quantifiable and you must cling to them with all your strength:

- **Risk**
- **Volatility**
- **Exposure**

There's very little to quantify, because, as we have said, the probability of success of a position is not quantifiable, the future cannot be predicted...

So, what can we quantify?

What do we rely on?

The only quantifiable things on which we must cling with all our strength are:

- Risk, meaning potential loss, i.e., how much we can lose in each position and in the long run.
- The volatility of the market, i.e., how much it moves, how much it fluctuates.
- Exposure, meaning how many positions are open and how exposed we are to the market.

These are the main things we can quantify and use as parameters.

WHY DOESN'T TECHNICAL ANALYSIS WORK?

Technical Analysis and Chart Analysis are not used to predict the future!

Many people (mistakenly) think that technical analysis serves to predict what the market will do tomorrow or in the next hours.

It is not like that!

Obviously, there is always a predictive component in Trading: if we are investing in something, it's because we believe that it will be worth more over time.

If, for example, we invest in Bitcoin, it's because we believe it will become more valuable in the future.

Also from a cumulative point of view, when we want to buy this other currency because we believe it will become valuable in the next few years, we are accumulating.

This, however, is not trading!

Let's always make this distinction: technical analysis is not for saying "The ascending triangle will be bullish!". No!

This is an improper use of the technical analysis.

Supports, resistances and indicators give a perspective on the market, on how to open favorable positions, identify trends, patterns, key levels and targets.

Technical analysis serves to have a clear perspective on the market and to be able to open a favorable position, identify trends, patterns and key prices.

It also allows to focus on targets from one side (the profit) and from the other (the loss).

Therefore, thanks to technical analysis, we can see how much gain we can have, and if the position will have a certain outcome.

For example, if we want to open a position on a breakout retest, we open it and then see how much space there is before the next resistance.

This is the space that allows us to calculate the possible reward or profit.

We do the same if it comes back down and we need to figure out where to place the stop loss. If we see that the stop loss is much more far away than the take profit, then we have an unfavorable position, since the risk is greater than the reward.

We have understood that technical analysis serves to have an overview of the position and quantify the exact risk by reading the chart... not to predict the future saying: "I open the position here, because it will happen this, technical analysis told me!".

Otherwise, perhaps it will be fine once or twice, then we make a mistake, we get angry and we say that technical analysis does not work (it's our fault instead, because we made an improper use of it).

A position is favorable when:

- **The risk is not exaggerated compared to the target.**
- **Historically it has had a positive outcome.**

When can we say that a position is favorable?

When the risk is not exaggerated compared to the target and when historically it has been successful.

"Historically it has been successful" means that we have to keep track of our positions over time, see which ones go one way and which ones another and accumulate as much data as possible on them.

So, next time we open a position, we will be able to evaluate how it went in the past and understand if it could be favorable or not based on the history.

The more data the better.

MINIMISE RISK

This is a very important concept which should be repeated ad nauseam!

Supposing we will only open favorable positions, the key issue shifts.

Let's start with the concept that we want every position we open to be favorable.

We make our technical analysis and open positions only where the analysis frames favorable positions and the history confirms it.

We have to shift the key problem a little because we no longer wonder how much to earn and how much to put in... that is something we have to define upstream.

The only thing we don't know is the risk to be reduced.

How to do it? How to safeguard the capital?

Problem: reducing the risk as much as possible.

- **Position risk - Technical analysis**
- **Capital risk -?**
- **Bankruptcy risk - ?**

This is the first thing to do in every position we open.

There are three types of risk:

- Individual position risk: i.e., the risk of losing the expected capital in that position. The technical analysis helps us to quantify and reduce it.
- Capital risk: the risk of how much capital we are going to lose in the various positions.

Therefore, if we have associated to a position a certain capital to lose and to another one a different figure, the whole of the positions gives us the capital risk.

Obviously, this risk is to be mitigated, and Money Management, which we will see better later on, can help us to do that.

- Bankruptcy risk: the risk to make the same mistake as the capital risk but in the long run, that is the risk to drain our account completely.

Also here, Risk Management will come to our aid.

THE RIGHT OPERATION

It is essential to frame an operation that goes well with one's character.

The personal psychological factor is fundamental.

We must be at ease with the Trading we do, otherwise we will be overwhelmed by emotionality.

We must understand on which time frame to operate and which type of positions we can manage better.

We mustn't improvise as intraday traders if we get anxious!

Better to use a wider time frame.

This is why there is no universal strategy.

We may be better off watching the market 5 times a day and adjusting our trades all 5 times, using a daily timer.

Someone else could be better off operating on 30-minute time frames, exploiting the short movements, because s/he knows how to set well the stop loss and the take profit on those movements.

All this is personal, there is no right or wrong.

There is what works best for you. And it is exactly for this reason that it does not have sense to copy what someone else does.

STRATEGY AND PLANNING

Therefore, what we have to do is to plan.

Plan everything down to the last detail and quantify the quantifiable.

Without a plan you will get nowhere.

We should leave as little room as possible for improvisation, especially at the beginning.

We define our parameters of Risk Management, that is how much to risk for Trade, how much to risk if we make three losses in row, what to modify, where to put the stop loss and the take profit, which setup to use, etc.

At this point, we must follow literally what we have defined, otherwise we move away from our initial strategy and introduce unmeasurable variables and we do not succeed in keeping trace of our data and self-evaluating.

When you have enough experience, you will be more flexible.

If you find yourself in front of a very interesting position (because historically it gives more favorable results), at that point you can decide to risk a little more capital.

This reasoning, however, should not be made at the beginning, when you have no idea of anything.

You can do it when you have a lot of experience and years of data.

Exclude emotionality and stick to the strategies used.

You have to learn to suffer losses, even in series.

This is the ABC.

It's a repetition, but it's essential to keep it in mind!

If you lose two or three times in a row and you say to yourself "No, nothing works anymore... I'm going to move the stop loss... I'm going to wait to break-even as soon as the trade starts to improve...!" etc. etc., you will be completely off track, because you'll end up getting everything wrong.

You'll have to learn to suffer losses in series too, because it will happen sooner or later!

Trading is also made of series of losses and suffering them is bad.

It hurts.

Believe me, getting 4 or 5 stop losses in a row hurts your capital and yourself, because it's always difficult to say "I was wrong".

But it's part of the game.

Therefore, you must always be objective and understand that losses are physiological and that the strategy continues to work... there are simply moments of "bad luck".

On the other hand, when the fundamental conditions of the market are changed (long-term trend inversions, higher or lower volatility or very different volumes etc.), it is necessary to be objective and understand that the strategy should be modified following a plan.

WINNING OPERATION

From this first chapter I would like you to understand this: we have to follow this scheme.

PART 1: Defining time horizons and setting objectives.

Start defining your goals and strategy, then try to acquire the basic concepts and understand what you can and cannot achieve.

Once you understand this (which was the purpose of the first chapter), you will already be way ahead of most people who "do trading".

Ask yourself:

Do I want to invest in the long run?

Do I want to speculate?

How much do I want to invest?

How much do I want to speculate?

You need to have this extremely clear in your mind and not say "Yeah... In 1 or 2 years we'll see what happens...".

No!

You need to set extremely clear objectives. We will see this very soon.

PART 2: Defining operation.

The most concrete and raw part: building a portfolio, based on the objectives defined a priori;

Set up a risk management strategy;

Defining individual positions: only trade after defining portfolio and strategy.

PART 3: Self-assessment and adaptation.

Constantly evaluate your results by noting and quantifying them.

It is essential to constantly rebalance operation in favor of the best performances, limiting the worst ones: this is the purpose of self-assessment.

Have a little more confidence and awareness of what you are doing.

We have reached the end of this first chapter; I hope it has been useful to you and I hope to have transmitted to you the fundamental concepts on which to construct a profitable strategy.

Let's remember that the mindset is the truth.

Feet on the ground and clear ideas are the basics and without them you cannot even start.

VOCABULARY OF
THE CRYPTO TRADER

Here we are at the second chapter of the path dedicated to those who want to learn to develop independently a profitable trading strategy over the long term, thus differentiating themselves from the mass of "Traders" who focus on the short term instead, on making too much profit in a short time and on single positions rather than on the overview of their portfolio.

In the first chapter we have built the foundations, getting rid of the wrong preconceptions and setting the right mindset towards a long-term profitability and a more strategic vision of Trading itself.

In this chapter we will understand the meaning of some fundamental terms regarding the different aspects of Trading, from buying and selling to the market, up to the chart analysis and operation.

We will use a vocabulary and a glossary where we take the term, define it and exploit it, trying to understand the concept behind the term itself.

These are basic concepts about the market, chart reading and operation.

THE CORRECT TERMINOLOGY

The purpose of this chapter is to start from the terms, from the words that are at the base of the Trading world, concerning operation, exchanges, chart analysis, candlesticks...in short, some terms useful to understand what is being said when some analysis is made or some process is explained.

Starting from the definition of the words, we will also define the concepts that gravitate around them, in order to give you a basic knowledge of those activities that represent the pillars of Trading itself.

Once we know these terms and concepts, we can work on them in a more advanced way, going deeper in the operation, in the strategies and in what will come later.

SUPPLY AND DEMAND

Understanding the market mechanism is absolutely fundamental and the relationship between supply and demand is what makes the price, what makes the market.

Order book

The market can be represented on every platform and on every Exchange (in this case the chart is from Binance).

What is an Order book?

It is a visual representation, a kind of table showing supply and demand.

At the bottom, green-colored, we have the demand (Bids) while at the top, red-colored, we have the supply (Asks).

This is the liquidity that this market has.

In the middle, we have the so called "Last Price", that is the last price at which a purchase, a sale or a negotiation was made.

The two prices that are closer to the center of the Order book, that is the Last Price, are the so-called "Market Prices"; these are different between supply and demand, and cannot meet each other because, if supply and demand met, we would have a negotiation.

In liquidity, on the other hand, there must always be a minimum difference between supply and demand, which is defined as the "spread".

The lowest price of the offer (in the graph it is the last number in red, close to the Market Price) will be the one at which we will buy, in case we buy at market.

On the contrary, in the demand, we must consider the highest price (represented in green, at the top of the list) at which we will sell, if we sell at market.

Clearly, the more demand or supply there is, the more difficult it will be to move the price in one direction or another.

Why?

Let's imagine that we have a lot of supply, many people want to sell and have placed their sell orders at different prices which are very high.

It's necessary that someone at market buys from all those sell orders, so that the price can go up.

The more people buy, the higher it goes up.

If, however, there are "walls" for sale it will be difficult to "eat" them and make the price go up.

Similarly, when there is a lot of demand, it will take even more supply to meet all the demand and lower the price accordingly. Indeed, the price is defined by the balance between supply and demand.

Depth chart

The graphical representation, even if not in tabular form, is called Depth Chart and shows the depth of the market (supply side and demand side) in the form of a line.

If we see a "green wall" on the left (usually the price axis starts from zero and goes forward), or a "wall" for sale on the right, it means that there is a lot of demand or supply. Therefore, it will be easier or more difficult (more difficult if the wall is high) to move the price in that direction.

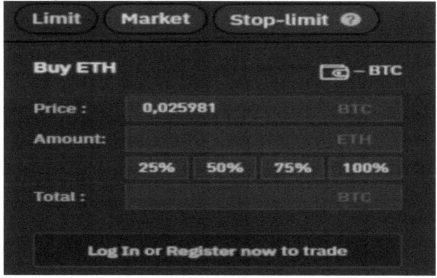

ORDERS

There are three types of orders: Limit, Market and Stop.

What is the difference between these and how do they interact with the market?

Limit Order

It is the most used and it is a buy or sell order (Limit Buy or Limit Sell) that is placed inside the Order book (creating liquidity in this) at a price that we define (Limit Price). Returning to the example above and taking this situation as an example, if we wanted to enter a buy order at 0.025990 Bitcoins, we would create a Limit Buy with Limit Price at 0.0025990 and this automatically ends up in the demand of the Order book (if it were a Limit Sell, it would end up in the offer).

Be careful: the Limit Price must be lower than the Market Price!

If we make a buy order with a price that is higher than the Market Price in purchase, we satisfy, in reality, an offer.

We make a Market Order and therefore it becomes a different order.

On the contrary, the Limit Price must be higher than the Market Price in sale.

If we put a Limit Sell that is lower, we will satisfy a Market Order.

The Limit Order makes us Market Makers because we create liquidity, that is to say we create the market.

Market Order

It is an order immediately made at Market Price.

For example, if we make a Market Buy at 0.02599, we will pick from the Market Price in purchase (the last one in red) from the lowest offer.

In other words, if our Market Buy is immense in volume, then we will pick from the lowest price of the offer.

When this part of the order is completed, we will go to the higher price and so on.

If we buy a lot, we will raise the price a bit, because we satisfy a lot of supply.

Conversely, if we sell at market, we will sell to demand at a higher price.

So, as we gradually satisfy all of it, we make the price go down.

These are the two sides of the market:

– Market Makers, we are dealing with Limit Orders if we create liquidity.

– Market Takers when we take advantage of the liquidity of others and make Market Orders.

Stop Order

This is a particular case, let's say a conditional order.

We have to define, in addition to the Limit Price (if we want to do it at a Stop Limit) or otherwise we can also do a Stop Market and we have to define the Stop Price, a threshold price that the Last Price will have to cross in order to trigger our order.

Let's take a step back and try to understand better.

We can obviously make a Buy or Sell order.

If we want to make a Stop Buy (a buy order), we have to put a Stop Price which is higher than the Last Price.

So, if the Last Price rises until it exceeds our Stop Price, then the Stop Buy is placed.

It can be a Stop Limit Buy, which in that case will place in the Order book a Limit Buy, or a Stop Market Buy, which will buy at market at the best possible offer.

On the other hand, if the order has a Stop Sell, it works the other way around: if the Last Price drops below the Stop Price, our order is triggered and can go to the Order book or buy from the available liquidity.

These are the basic order types. Now let's take a step forward and enter the world of derivatives and Margin Trading.

DERIVATIVES AND MARGIN TRADING

By derivatives we mean for example futures and options.

Now, in reality, I do not want to define derivative contracts because it is a more advanced concept, I only want to define the ABC of Margin Trading and Leveraged Trading of derivative contracts (when we talk about long or short liquidation and things like that, just to be clear).

Margin Trading: why is it called that?

Because we use a portion of the total position to trade.

Concrete example: we use $100 to open a $1000 position.

These $100 that we put in is called margin, while we borrow the remaining $900 from someone else or from the Exchange itself. These make the value of our position much greater than what we put in.

This position is called "leveraged."

The leverage is the size of the open position divided by the capital used for the margin.

So, in the $100 example, if we open a $1000 position the leverage is X10, because 1000 is equal to 10 times 100.

Therefore, we can trade Long or Short: Long is a position that produces profit if the market goes up, Short is a position that produces profit if the market goes down.

So, you can earn from any type of movement.

The image on the previous page is taken from the Exchange "Bitmex", one of the most famous for Margin Trading (Derivative trading).

What are the advantages and disadvantages of Leveraged Trading?

The gains are amplified, because we spend $100 but, if the market rises, we gain as if we had spent $1000.

The disadvantage is that if the market goes down the loss is extremely amplified, up to the limit case: the liquidation, or Margin call, if the market goes down so much as to zero the margin, then our position is closed and we are left with $0.

In the example we gave, if we put in $100 to open a $1000 position, we have to calculate how much the market has to go down (i.e., in case a Long position is opened) to lose $100, to lose all our margin and how much 10% is (10% of 1000 is 100).

So, if the market goes down by 10%, having opened a $1000 position, we lose $100. We lose the margin, go into liquidation and our position is closed.

The Liquidation Price is precisely the Last Price at which liquidation is triggered.

The higher the leverage, the closer the entry price.

Assuming the upper limit of Bitmex, we open a position with leverage 100X: if the market goes contrary to our 1% position, our margin is burned completely and we go into liquidation.

So, be careful! The pros and cons of leverage are basically these and you have to be very careful and plan everything ahead.

GRAPHICAL ANALYSIS 1 – CANDLES

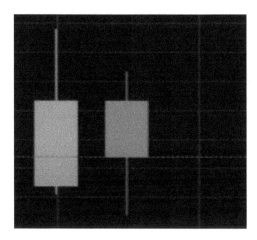

Let's try to understand the terminology at the basis of chart reading, starting from the functional unit of the chart which is the "Japanese candlestick".

<u>Open, Close, High and Low: opening, closing, maximum and minimum of the candle.</u>

The four parameters are also called O - C - H - L.

There are two types of candles:

- The bullish candle (in green) when the closing is greater than the opening.
- The bearish candlestick (in red) when the closing is lower than the opening.

Where are the Open, Close, High and Low in this chart?

In the green candlestick, we have the Open at the bottom and the Close at the top because we have a bullish movement. High and Low are always the absolute maximum and minimum.

In the red candlestick, the Open and Close are inverted, because it is a bearish candlestick. Maximum and minimum are always absolute.

<u>Real Body and Shadows</u>

Let's define the inner and outer part of the candlestick.

The inner part is defined Real Body and is between the opening and closing.

On the other hand, the Shadows are the external tips of the Real Body, and can be:

- Upper Shadow: between the maximum and the opening or closing depending on the direction.
- Lower Shadow: between the minimum and the opening or closing depending on the direction.

Volume

In addition to the candle that shows us the price (or Price Action: the price movement) we have another fundamental parameter in the chart, that is the volume.

Volume is defined as the countervalue that is moved in a candlestick.

It is represented at the bottom of the histogram or with a horizontal line and can be red or green.

GRAPHICAL ANALYSIS 2 – MOVEMENTS

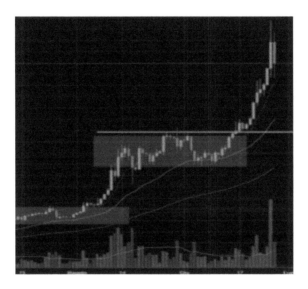

There are different types of movements and here I will explain the basic ones.

<u>Cluster and Lateralization</u>

Horizontal movements within a narrow area. In the chart they are represented in green.

(This is Bitcoin at its most "bullish" phase!)

<u>Impulses</u>

Usually found between one lateralization and the other. They tend to be vertical.

<u>Higher High and Lower Low</u>

• Higher High: a maximum which is higher than the previous one.

• Lower low: a minimum which is lower than the previous one.

Higher high, Lower low, Lower high and Higher Low define the Trend.

<u>Trend</u>

Actually, there are many ways to define a Trend.

The Trend is simply the direction of the market.

It strongly depends on the time frame observed.

If we look at a 1-minute time frame, the trend is different, because it is much faster, and changes much faster.

A trend can be Bullish or Bearish depending on the direction:

● Bullish: also called Uptrend (can be found in the Higher highs and Higher lows).

● Bearish: or Downtrend (if we have Lower highs and Lower lows).

Little-known fact:

Why are they called Bullish and Bearish?

Because the bull gores from the bottom to the top (bullish movement), while the bear hits with its paws from the top to the bottom (bearish movement).

<u>Retracement</u>

A movement against trend or a corrective move, also called "countermovement". Usually, the more impulses are found on one side, the more likely it is that there will be a retracement afterwards.

The retracement is intended to reverse part of this movement and eventually to continue the Trend.

GRAPHICAL ANALYSIS 3 – KEY LEVELS

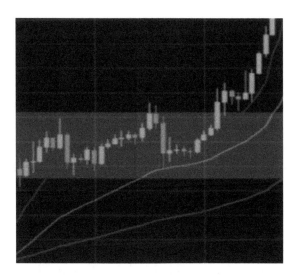

Analyzing the movements more closely (a middle way between the candle and the chart as a whole), we can define the key levels.

The key levels are the ones to highlight and on which we should base our positions because a Trader usually relies precisely on price levels.

<u>Support and Resistance</u>

These are two sides of the same coin.

A support is a price that hinders the descent: in the chart you will notice that it has bounced several times on the base of the rectangle and it has never been violated downwards.

On the contrary, a resistance is a price that hinders the rise (high base of the rectangle).

Clearly the support, if violated, can become a resistance.

Violated supports that become resistances are called Support to Resistance Flip, but this is a somewhat more advanced concept that we will see in the setups.

The same goes for the resistance.

A price that hinders a rise becomes a support.

<u>Break</u>

It can be a Breakout if the break is bullish or a Breakdown if it is bearish.

In the case of our chart, we had a Breakout retest, i.e. the return to a support and resistance level on the opposite side.

Patterns

They are repeatable characterizable formations.

Some of them are triangles, some are W, double minimums, double maximums, etc. etc.

As they are characterizable formations, we say what they must satisfy and above all what the break conditions are (these are the most important things because they give a cue for operation) and we identify them on the various Time frames, on the various charts, therefore they are repeatable.

Traps

They are false breaks and can be divided in:

● Bull Trap: false Breakout.

One sees the Breakout, buys and maybe that Breakout is false.

Immediately after that, it is refuted and therefore one gets screwed, because s/he bought thinking to have a Breakout and in reality it does not happen.

● Bear Trap: false Breakdown.

Maybe one sells or goes short for a breakdown, but then it is refuted immediately.

GRAPHICAL ANALYSIS 4 – ANOMALIES

We could write a book on this topic, but I have chosen 4 anomalies:

Pump/Dump

- Pump is a sudden increase, a very long green candlestick with crazy volumes;
- Dump is a very long red candlestick with crazy volumes.

"Pump and Dump" is a pattern that basically aims to make the price rise very suddenly, and then sell off and lower it immediately.

You will see a green candlestick and, immediately after that, a red one that brings the price more or less at par.

It is highly inadvisable to operate in these situations.

Spike

A very long shadow, which signals the sudden movement of the price, immediately rejected.

Stop Hunting

A sudden, short and intense movement, aimed at triggering massive Stop Orders. Maybe it is a bit difficult to understand, but let's imagine we are a whale with huge capital and we want to manipulate the price.

We are very close to a support or resistance and we can imagine that under that support is the Stop Sell.

If we can push the price up to there, selling off at market a lot, meeting the demand, and lowering the price to below the minimum support, at that point we also trigger their Stop Orders, lowering the price even more.

In fact, a triggered Stop Order is another sell order that meets more demand and lowers the price even more.

This way we are obviously able to buy at an even lower price.

Stop hunting has this purpose: to trigger Stop Orders.

It is a manipulative movement aimed at triggering Stop Orders.

Bart

Formation similar to the head of Bart Simpson characterized by impulse, minimum lateralization and impulse opposite to the first one.

Usually, this Pattern is drawn because of the Stop Hunting, because a series of Stops are triggered and make the price rise.

Suppose the Stop buys make the price go up, then nothing happens anymore and maybe around that lateralization, again, liquidity forms on one side and the Stop Orders on the other side.

Immediately manipulating, the price is lowered again and another collapse happens due to the domino effect of the Stop Orders.

When there is little "organic" movement, you usually see many Barts.

OPERATION 1 - SINGLE POSITION

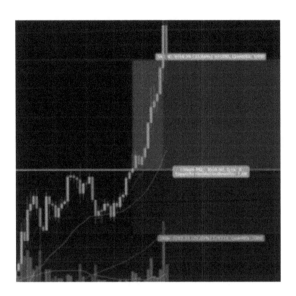

How can you define a position?

You usually open it by seeing particular configurations.

A Trader must operate on specific setups, not randomly.

Setup

It must be defined obsessively.

We must have our Setups on which to operate, leaving the minimum to chance.

It must be pretty schematic and defined.

Entry Price

Entry level, it can be Long or Short.

Stop Loss

Fundamental, always to be defined.

I will dedicate an entire chapter only to the Stop Loss.

It defines the price at which we close the position at a loss.

If the market pushes the price up to there, it means that our setup is invalidated and we were wrong, so we have to admit our mistake and cut our losses.

Always cut losses, never hold open positions hoping that sooner or later they will reverse.

Take profit

Closing a position at a profit.

The target of our position, if it goes well, is the take profit.

It is chosen according to various parameters and it all depends on the setup.

Risk

Capital at risk, that is the capital lost if the Stop Loss is triggered.

It must be clearly defined before opening the position, because we need to know how much to risk.

Reward

Net gain in case of Take profit.

R/R - Risk/Reward

Risk to Reward Ratio, which is the ratio between profit and risk capital.

The higher it is, the more favorable the Trade.

In this case we gain 1.68 times the risk capital and, if the Trading goes to Stop Loss, we lose only the risk capital.

On the other hand, the larger the Stop Loss is, the larger the Take Profit must be in order to gain more than we could lose.

Obviously, there is no rule that says what the best Risk to Reward Ratio is; it all depends on the strategy and we will talk about it in a very exhaustive way in the future.

For example, if we risk $100 per Trade, when our Trade goes into loss and reaches the Stop loss, we lose $100.

If, on the other hand, our trade goes to Take profit, we gain $168, so 1.68/ our risk capital.

PSYCHOLOGICAL AND EMOTIONAL MISTAKES: HOW TO AVOID THEM AND HOW TO AVOID LOSING MONEY

In the third chapter of part 1, we will do a short psychology lesson.

Specifically, this chapter will be about emotionality.

We will understand some common weaknesses of human nature which make us lose money.

What is the point of understanding them?

It serves to be aware of them, to take a step back and to overcome the problematic situation by rationalizing.

Rationalizing is the key in Trading.

You can rely neither on emotions, nor on instinct: you have to rationalize everything!

I know that the basics are boring, but starting from them you can build the most solid foundations on which you can then add the operation, which comes only after understanding the basic concepts.

This way profitability is easier to achieve and maintain consistently, which is our main goal.

Let's see what mistakes this unreliable emotionality leads us to make and, above all, how to overcome them.

EMOTIONAL TRAPS AND HOW TO AVOID THEM

Never be afraid to miss the train: in the markets there is no such thing as a train that never passes again. Especially in Trading.

If for once we miss a movement it doesn't matter, we can wait for the next one rather than running after the one in progress, which will surely result in a loss.

Let's deal with those more insidious mistakes to which we are induced by emotionality, in order to avoid them.

I have divided them into groups to address them all.

In my opinion, this is one of the main differences between the professional trader and the amateur trader: the amateur trader who approaches this world for the first time is not aware of these treacherous methods that our psyche has to alter the perception of reality; consequently, s/he doesn't realize and doesn't consider them.

Awareness is precisely the first step toward correcting the mistake.

By realizing that we are making a mistake, we can ask ourselves "Am I falling into that type of mistake? Yes!"

So we wait, take a step back and modify our operation.

THE 5 MAIN TYPES OF MISTAKES RELATED TO EMOTIONALITY (EMOTIONALITY + TRADING = LOSS)

The types of mistakes related to emotionality all lead to lose money because (I am telling you this beforehand) acting in the throes of emotions leads to lose money in every situation.

Ignore those who encourage you to inspire yourself, not to rationalize or go on instinct, because that's insanity.

These are the 5 things to avoid:

- **Giving personal assessments**
- **Being unable to admit mistakes**
- **Wanting to predict the market**
- **Wanting to make sense of any market movement**
- **Being influenced by others.**

1 - DO NOT GIVE PERSONAL ASSESSMENTS

Let's start with personal assessments.

The famous sentence "In my opinion it's because of this, but actually I'm positive about this asset so even if it goes down, I'll still buy it" is obviously a personal evaluation that risks putting us against the market and making us lose money.

The evaluations must derive only from the chart reading.

Be careful!

We are talking about trading; we are not talking about long-term investments or things like that.

We are talking about trading and, as such, trading must be "unbiased", that is free from personal preconceptions.

It is not good to have bias towards an asset, just because we like it.

If we really believe in an Altcoin because we like its design, but we are in a phase where Bitcoin dominus continues to rise, it's crazy to buy it blindly hoping it will rebound!

It might not happen and lead us to lose money.

Opening or holding open positions at a loss longer than necessary just because we expect something from news/events/fundamentals is absolutely wrong.

"Yeah, in a week there will be this event... there will be this news... there will be the release of a new version of the protocol...". NO!

"Yeah, I am at a loss, the setup is different from what I expected, but I will hold the open position anyway because I expect that this news will trigger this market reaction...". Terrible mistake.

This way we are giving our own evaluation, a personal evaluation to an event and, above all, to the market. The market is made up of many people, each of whom thinks differently.

So, we are also acting arrogantly by thinking that our vision of things is the correct one, that others will see it as we do and that, as a result, they will buy, driving up the price.

No! Be careful, this is a catastrophic mistake.

Solution: get an idea about the fundamentals of the projects and use it as a filter.

(Not to open or manage trades!)

Having an idea about the projects is a very good thing, you must study them and know what you are investing in.

But should this idea be used as a filter or to invest in the long run?

This is not Trading; this is long-term investment.

It is necessary to distinguish these two things and not in order to open or manage trades (which absolutely do not need personal evaluations).

Expecting something could mean chaos and therefore perhaps it is better not to even open positions because of relevant news or events.

Their outcome can be absolutely unpredictable.

2 - ADMIT WHEN YOU ARE WRONG

This aspect is really important, but for a proud person it's hard to admit mistakes.

In our case, it's really part of the game.

Trading is not a position, it's not being better than others at predicting what will happen but it's being better than others at managing risk and situations where you make mistakes or lose.

Managing losses with a clear mind during strategies that foresee a loss rate, an error rate greater than the gain rate: this makes a trader a good trader!

In such case, we are dealing with strategies that predict to make correct trades 40% of the time, but to make Stop Loss 60% of the time!

Obviously, these strategies will be profitable if, in that 40% of the time, our profit is much greater than what we lose in the other 60% of the time.

We are still profitable Traders.

That's why it's very important to manage losses and mistakes without being discouraged and without losing clarity of mind.

It is necessary to understand when the opened Trade has gone wrong and to take note of it as soon as possible.

Rebuttal Scenario - Stop Loss

At the very moment we open a position, we need to foresee a rebuttal scenario.

For example, we open a position on a setup (e.g., the Breakout of a resistance level and we open the retest that follows).

When does the Breakout get invalidated?

Maybe we leave some space and put the invalidation below the previous low, before the breakout (or we will have our reasons), but the important thing is that there is this invalidation scenario.

Otherwise, it means entering and hoping it goes well.

We should have clear in mind that when we are wrong, we have to cut our losses thanks to the stop loss.

Never hold an open position waiting for it to go back up, hoping that it will only take a little longer than expected.

This is another classic example.

Maybe we buy expecting a Breakout, but immediately after the Breakout, it turns out to be fake, there is a nice red candle that makes the price "dump" again below and we keep the position open.

Another clamorous mistake!

Hope never leads to good results.

You should be objective and cut the losses before they get worse.

Be careful: even if you close in stop loss, the Trade will be positive, because the stop loss has been touched anyway.

Never rely on luck, but always on setups and precise conditions.

Solution: always use the stop loss and
be able to reverse the Bias.

What is a Bias?

It is a predisposition to be bullish or bearish.

Sometimes the fact that our position is invalidated by the stop loss may suggest the opening of an opposite position.

3 - DO NOT PREDICT THE FUTURE

Already said on several occasions ...

It's a human and arrogant tendency:
thinking you have the situation under control and know what will happen.

Not predicting the future is difficult, because it is an innate tendency in people.

Everyone wants to predict the future and some people asked me "What is the point of not predicting the future if we are Traders and we earn money from market movements and from predicting market movements?".

No! Mistake!

The market is not rational, it does not obey mathematical laws and it is not
predictable, but only anticipatable.

To predict means to imagine what will happen in the future, to anticipate means to see that something is happening and go for it.

You do not gain from predicting market movements, while you gain from anticipating market movements.

For example, we see a Breakout, we know that an impulsive movement with volumes has formed, we wait for the price to retest the level from which it started and we enter, anticipating the movement that has just formed.

Obviously, anticipation always has a risk which is proportional to what we are anticipating.

Maximum risk, maximum gain. It is always like that.

So, it's very important to understand the concept of anticipation and the related risk, because the market is not rational.

There is no such thing as an ascending triangle breaking upwards 80% of the time.

No, it is pure madness!

It breaks upwards when it breaks upwards!

There are no patterns or graphical situations with a certain or almost
certain outcome.

Beware of those who predict prices or movements.

I have read crazy things on Telegram groups and the like: "The price will get there in 2025...!", "In 4 days there will be a 30% Pump!"

This can only be said by those who manipulate the market to the point of creating those Pumps, or by those who have already made a right prediction, or even two or three...but anyway, don't follow them!

The best Trader is not the one who predicts the best, because the prediction is a game of chance.

The best Trader is the one who can manage risk well over time, manage losses, gains, setups and have a result that is consistent over the long term.

Solution: operate on studied and planned setups.

We must operate on setups that we can manage, both in case of profit and error.

That means being able to recognize when we are wrong, manage the error (stop loss), manage the profit, where we place it, manage the risk and so on.

4 - DON'T SEEK THE REASON FOR EVERY MOVEMENT

Another human predisposition is to always want to know everything and give an explanation for everything!

The market is made by people. Many people. Each of them has its own reasons to buy or sell.

There are those who buy because they have seen a setup, those who buy because they have heard a piece of news, those who buy because they believe in the Asset and want to "hold it" for 5 years...

In short, everyone has his/her own reasons.

It is impossible to rationalize them all and adjust them thinking that there is something that pushes them to do so.

The price is given by supply and demand and demand can run out, even under the best conditions.

During the strong Trends on the rise, there is a lot of demand, then it progressively runs out because everybody goes Long (hoping as soon as possible), then the Trend is exacerbated and, at some point, people will go to Take profit and then the trend will be reversed moving the needle towards the offer against the demand.

Demand and offer are unpredictable, but observable.

Solution: do not seek fundamental reasons for the movements.

Movements are the result of supply and demand over time, so let's not always try to figure out when there is a movement that goes as expected.

We need to follow the flows and weigh positions and risks.

5 - DON'T BE INFLUENCED BY OTHERS' ANALYSIS

Everyone has their own opinions, and their own economic background, capital, character, experience, risk tolerance ...

Obviously, someone who invests $1000 will not reason in the same way as someone who invests 20 million, so it makes no sense to compare the analysis that the two people make.

Those who invest $1000 will be more inclined to risk, trying to have a greater profit in the face of a greater risk.

On the other hand, those who invest 20 million wishing to lower the risk (and consequently to lower the profit), try to preserve their capital.

There are no universal analyses.

Every analysis must always be accompanied by a rebuttal scenario, since there is no certainty in the future.

A well-done analysis is the bullish scenario, Long position, in the event that a certain movement happens allowing us to open an X type position, with X profit and X stop loss.

Solution: if you read an analysis that is different from the one you have predetermined, stick to yours.

If you read an analysis on Twitter, Facebook or Telegram but you don't agree, that's fine! Everyone has their own strategy, there is no right or wrong one, as long as it is thoughtful, well-calculated, and integrated into your strategy.

So, these are the concepts to consider when trading.

- Let's realize when we are falling into one of these five types of mistakes;
- Let's take a step back;
- Let's be self-critical, which is really important, in life and in Trading.

COGNITIVE DISSONANCE

This is a macro topic, extremely frequent in Trading, which occurs when there are dissonant thoughts that make us feel uncomfortable.

In general, human psychology works like this: we have an idea and something that is opposite to that idea comes to our mind (for example we are smoking and we think that smoking is bad for us).

In case of discomfort, the human mind reacts in 3 ways:

- It ignores it, eliminates it or avoids it;
- It minimizes it, altering its importance;
- It invents excuses in favor of its own idea.

Being biased in the market translates into losing money, because we do not have a clear mind on the situation (typical process of cognitive dissonance in the Trader).

Example 1:

- We are Bullish on Bitcoin;
- Bitcoin tracks a lower low with dump and very high volumes;
- After reading the most Bullish news on Bitcoin, we convince ourselves that we are right, thinking that the charts are not relevant.

Example 2:

- We are Bullish on Bitcoin;
- The position does not develop as expected and the setup is invalidated;
- Looking at the fundamentals of the coin, we think they are good and we decide that our position becomes long-term, hoping that sooner or later it will go back up.

This is a typical process of cognitive dissonance that, together with the 5 cases of emotional traps, represents 90% of the errors in which we are induced by our emotionality and our psychology.

So, I recommend what follows: if you feel that you are in this situation, take note of it and try to be self-critical.

Go and look for the origin of that error and be more confident about your strategy.

Be as mathematical and rational as possible.

THE CONCEPT OF RISK

Trading gives life lessons and you will often read about my comparisons between the attitudes to adopt in trading and in life.

Learning to manage your emotions, risks and certain types of situations in the market is extremely valuable in life as well.

And I'm sure that once you get 100% into this perspective (if you haven't already), you will be able to take some concepts on board.

In this fourth chapter, we will take this aspect to the next level because we will deal with a concept that we face many times in life and continuously in trading every time we open a position, create a strategy and operate on the markets.

Risking is part of the Trader's job.

Every choice we make involves a risk.

There is no such thing as security, this is an outdated concept in a world that continues to change. As Heraclitus said "Existence is a continuous flow" and opposing this flow means falling behind.

Trying to oppose risk means precisely opposing this flow.

Being able to control and manage risk, therefore, distinguishes in both contexts those who can succeed from those who cannot.

Those who can manipulate risk in their favor, control it, quantify it and weigh it will have a much better chance of success.

Those who avoid it or expose themselves to exaggerated risk, will end up falling behind or going bankrupt!

INTRODUCTION TO RISK

In life we are always taught to avoid risk and always play it safe.
Now, that's a recipe for mediocrity!

Clearly not meant in the derogatory sense, mediocrity is not to be despised.

Mediocrity is part of human nature and there are those who want to remain in their comfort zone, and there is absolutely nothing wrong with that.

However, in Trading, this attitude is not good.

If you are a person who wants to play it safe, take a step back and give up.

Cryptocurrencies and Trading are a risky market by definition.

Any action that can lead to big results and/or achievements always has a related risk.

In order to achieve ambitious goals, you have to take risks.

Risk involves the possibility of failure. However, being able to put in sequence different risky situations by managing them intelligently, allows us (over the long term and if we are consistent enough) to achieve our results.

Offsetting risk

This is a universal law that applies both in life and in the markets.

It is necessary to calculate and weigh the risk of one's actions.

That means being able to rationalize in an extreme way, leaving aside emotionality and the most instinctive part of us.

In Trading and in the markets, risk translates into extremely quantifiable monetary terms.

We will have gains and losses at every operation.

So, we must be able to quantify the parameters that tell us how much we are risking.

Try to channel the risk and look for the optimal situation.

DECLINATION OF RISK IN THE MARKETS

I have declined risk into these four categories:

- **Capital Risk:**

How much capital do we lose if our Trade goes to Stop Loss?

- **Position Risk:**

How likely is it that our trade will go to Stop Loss?

- **Portfolio Risk:**

How likely is it that our portfolio will suffer a significant loss?

- **Bankruptcy Risk:**

How likely is it that our portfolio will go to zero?

CAPITAL RISK

Capital risk, also referred to as "R", is a key parameter and must be chosen in an extremely thoughtful way.

How much capital do we risk in each operation we do?

It can vary over time depending on what happens and directly influences the potential profit.

The more risks, the more gains in all situations.

The more capital we risk, the greater the net profit will be.

It is convenient to measure "R" as a percentage of the speculative portfolio.

The capital at risk depends on our availability of capital and therefore is measured as a percentage.

For example: if the market goes up by 10% and we have invested 10, we will earn 1.

If we put in 100, we will earn 10.

Very trivial.

The decision of the capital at risk depends on many factors.

To determine it, we need to consider the total Equity, type of position, willingness to take risk, time frame, etc...

For example, with a more anticipatory or lower time frame position, we want to risk a little less.

However, take on board the idea that the decision of the capital at risk doesn't have to be fixed in time, it is better to measure it as a percentage of your own Equity and it depends on several factors. The important thing is to think about it, define it clearly before opening the position and define a strategy for managing capital at risk.

Risk to Reward Ratio:

The Risk to Reward ratio is the ratio between potential profit and R, the only parameter that tells us how much we can gain and how much we can lose in certain positions.

We said that in a Trade we want to commit R, our capital at risk that we have predefined.

It will be lost in case the position goes to stop loss (which we have defined previously).

In the case of our chart, being a short position, this will happen when it exceeds the old maximum.

In this case R is 1.63, which means that if our position goes into profit, we will earn 1.63 times the capital at risk we have predefined.

This means defining the totality of a position.

A higher R/R doesn't necessarily mean a better strategy or position.

R/R and Win Rate

Let's introduce the concept of win rate, which is the percentage of trades closed in profit.

Let's suppose that we have the history of our trades and we are calculating how many have gone into profit and how many have not.

The win rate doesn't have to be necessarily greater than 50% to have an Equity that increases over time.

For example: a trader makes 5 trades, with an average R/R of 2.

- if s/he goes into profit, s/he gains 2R;
- if s/he goes to stop loss, s/he loses R.

If s/he had 2 trades in profit and 3 trades in loss, his/her Win Rate would be less than 50% (2 out of 5, then 40%).

But what is the final result?

2 trades in profit produced 2R each, that is 4R.

From this we must subtract the 3R of the loss.

So, 4R - 3R = 1R of Profit!

On the contrary: a trader makes 5 trades, with an average R/R of 0.6.

Exactly the same situation, i.e., with 2 trades in profit and 3 in loss.

The final result will be 3 X 0.6R - 2R = 0.2R of Loss!

The Win Rate necessary to the break-even is equal to 100/(R/R Average +1).

To obtain the Break-even (i.e., the parity) we must use this formula.

On the basis of the first example in profit: 100/(2+1) = 100/3 = 33.333333%

In the case of loss: 100/(0.6+1) = 100/1.6 = 62.5%

The Win Rate is inversely proportional to the R/R.

If we try to open positions with a higher R/R (more profitable if they go into profit) than the capital at risk, this drastically lowers our Win Rate.

If we want to keep the Win Reward higher, we usually have to reduce the R/R.

Of course, the R/R must be decided by technical analysis.

POSITION RISK

Every trade allows for the possibility of error.

Position risk is the acceptance of reality: there is no certain outcome and you cannot predict the future.

It involves, with historical data at the ready (our performance, win rates and every documented position), turning the scale in our favor.

The position risk is usually inversely proportional to the win rate.

"Position risk" and "Win Rate" are two terms which can be easily interchanged and are directly proportional.

Let's think about a situation of a high R, with a very anticipatory position, perhaps before the Breakout, under a resistance.

If we manage to put a tighter stop loss, we will have a higher R/R but a much higher position risk and consequently on N positions we will have a lower win rate.

This happens because it is much more likely that a stop hunting or something like that can invalidate our stop loss.

On the contrary, more cautious positions, a lower R/R, a wider stop loss and a lower position risk will ensure us a higher Win Rate.

The only way to estimate the position risk is the history.

Since there is no quantifiable probability, nor a number, the only way to calculate the PR (Position Risk) is the history.

We will use an empirical method, by backtesting (if we use a mechanical strategy, a programmed trading system) or by a Trading Journal (from our empirical win rate data).

We will evaluate how successful we have been with the different types of positions in the past and estimate WR and PR for each strategy, which we will then evaluate over time.

PORTFOLIO RISK AND BANKRUPTCY RISK

Let's finish the discussion on risk by talking about portfolio risk and bankruptcy risk.

These are the two worst things ever.

From the single position, we will move to the set of positions that make up our portfolio.

It is important to keep track of our capital, measuring it in the base currency.

Equity Line

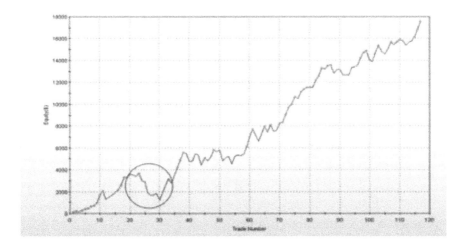

The Equity Line is a graph of our capital over time, it represents how the capital varies over time.

As you can see in the graph, each dot is a Trade executed.

On the X axis there is the number of trades, on the Y axis there is the profit in dollars or the currency we want.

It serves to keep track of the trend of our capital over time measuring it in the Base Currency, which is the currency on which we want to profit.

Example: Base currency: Dollars (Y axis).

Drawdown

We need to keep track of the drawdown phases: the significant decreasing phases of equity.

They are part of the game, there is no trading without drawdown phases.

This is the most psychologically difficult part to manage.

Sometimes continuing to trade can become really frustrating.

Minimizing Drawdown phases

We must learn to manage these phases in terms of extent and over time. Here's how to:

- Limit concurrent exposure on correlated assets

(Divide and diversify your positions);

- Limit the counter-trend exposure

(Statistically riskier);

- Limit exposure to Low Time frame

(Open few positions at a time to avoid stop loss);

- Diversify positions as much as possible;
- Reduce R in case of sequential losses

(Create an R/R reduction policy);

- Evaluate the exclusion (temporary or definitive) of systems or strategies not relevant to the current market phase

(Adapt to the market);

- Evaluate an operational pause in case of psychological conditions which are not optimal for trading (anger, fatigue, lack of clear-headedness, etc. ...)

VOLATILITY AND OPTIMIZATION OF STRATEGIES

In this chapter we will talk about volatility.

Volatility is a very important concept in trading because it must influence the operation itself.

Depending on the volatility conditions of the market we should adopt a different approach.

Not all market phases work the same, in fact now we will talk about this.

Let's start from the concept of market as a set of people.

As such, it obeys the laws of group and mass psychology.

We will see how this can directly affect our operation in order to make trades with knowledge, so that they are extremely profitable and low risk.

VOLATILITY AND MARKET PHASES

These two elements are closely intertwined and dependent on each other.

We will examine this link; we will try to understand the market phase in which we are thanks to the volatility measurement and consequently we will learn to regulate our operation according to the current phase.

Nowadays, we frame the market as what it is: a group phenomenon.

It's a social phenomenon that involves the participation of a mass of people (investors, institutions, Traders, etc...) and as such it involves some dynamics that are typical of groups and masses.

Volatility in the context of the market is what quantifies how agitated this group is, how much it participates, how much excitement there is in this group of actors that make the price.

This concept makes us understand many things about the current situation and adapt the strategy to be applied.

WHAT IS VOLATILITY?

Volatility: measure of the price changes over time, averaged over a certain period.

In a nutshell, volatility measures how much the price rises and falls in a sudden and wide way during a variable period of time (30 days, 6 months, 1 year, etc.).

This calculation, in my opinion, is not very useful for practical purposes.

The standard deviation of the price from the average

The definition of volatility that I prefer is this one, and when I talk about volatility, I precisely mean the standard deviation of the price from the average.

The purpose of volatility analysis is to define the market phase.

Analyzing volatility is useful to understand in which market phase we are and if the market is in Trading range or Trending:

- Trading range: contraction/squeezing;
- Trending: expansion.

Each phase is better suited for different methodologies.

HOW TO MEASURE VOLATILITY

There are two indicators that I prefer:

Bollinger Bands

The Bollinger Bands Width (or BBW) is that indicator which has at its center the simple moving average, at the sides of which we find two bands equidistant from the average. These represent two standard deviations of the price from the average.

In short, this tells exactly how much standard deviation there is in the price from its average.

In the presence of very wide Bollinger Bands or during an expansion phase, we have a high BBW. When it is low, we are dealing with a contraction BBW. That is, high volatility and low volatility.

Indicator delay

There is no such thing as a perfect indicator.

Its main flaw is the delay.

Being an indicator based on a weighted average of 20 previous samples, it always gives a delayed signal.

From experience, I don't recommend lowering the number of samples on which the Bollinger Bands and their width are calculated.

I'd rather integrate the analysis of a Time frame with the analysis of sub-time frames (underlying Time Frames).

For example, if by doing an analysis on the daily Time Frame we see some strange movement in the Price Action (even if it is not yet clearly reflected by Bollinger Bands and volatility), we could check 2-4 hour time frames to try to better understand the current phase (if there has been some breakout, some beginning of volatility, etc.).

The application of this type of analysis makes little sense, in my opinion, on time frames wider than the daily one, because cryptocurrencies are already an extremely volatile and very noisy market and all this noise is mediated within the indicator.

If analyzed in a time frame wider than the daily one (24h), it would be useless.

Average True Range

This is another useful indicator to quantify volatility.

While BBWs tell us about the standard deviation from the average, the average true range is the average range in which the price moves.

So, if you use an automatic trading system (a BOT, for example), the average true range will help you to define the stop loss.

VOLATILITY AND GROUP PSYCHOLOGY

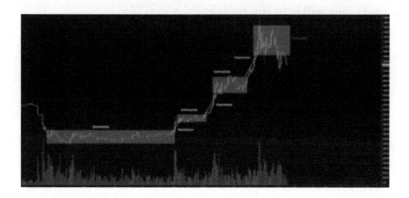

This chart is nothing but the movement of Bitcoin from the bottom to the top of $14,000.

As you can see, we have an alternation of contractions and expansions.

We notice long and tight contractions with low volumes, but also short impulsive expansions with high volumes.

They are really one the opposite of the other!

This reflects group psychology.

Any group phenomenon, whether in the animal or human world, works like this.

EXAMPLE:

Imagine the stages of a fight.

1. The first character starts to provoke a group of people;
2. The second character reacts;
3. A fight breaks out between several people (phase of maximum excitement or expansion);
4. Someone backs out or gets tired (contraction phase).

The phase of high excitement cannot last long: this shows the cyclical nature of any group phenomenon.

In the case of trading, in the market, which is a group phenomenon, a short phase of impulsive expansion is always followed by a contraction, which will be followed by another expansion and another contraction and so on, until the movement as a whole is exhausted.

So, there's an alternation between:

Expansion: impulsive movement, supported by volumes;

Contraction: slow movement, little wide and prolonged.

The last movement you see in the chart is an anomalous movement.

It is neither a contraction, nor an expansion.

I have called it **"turbulence"** and it can be defined as a mixture of the two movements, wide and chaotic, triggered by two opposite and close impulses.

This is because the longer a trend lasts, the more it is exacerbated and the more difficult it becomes to have a contraction phase.

The "turbulence" is a kind of contraction which, however, contains an expansive movement and that makes it result in a chaotic phase.

Usually, the moment of turbulence consists in the exasperation of the trend in progress and may result in a correction or reversal of the movement.

When there are symptoms of turbulence, it is better to back out!

To summarize:

Turbulence = peak of the trend

FRACTAL NATURE OF MARKET PHASES

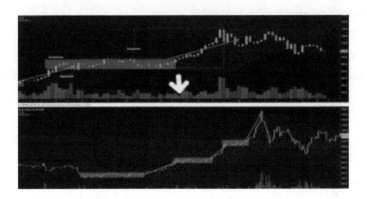

Each time frame that we observe contains structures that repeat themselves.

If we divide the daily time frame and consider only a 4-hour section, we will notice the repetition and alternation of contraction and expansion, like sub-phases.

Sub-time frame analysis

In the previous chart you can see an expansion phase in the daily time frame (top chart).

If we select a 4-hour time frame, that phase contains sub-phases (contraction and expansion).

In the bottom chart you can see the beginning of the expansive movement in a very marked way within the selected time frame, which could not be perceived in the daily chart instead.

This is because a movement always starts from the lowest time frames and propagates to the highest ones.

On the time frame we can see a turbulence, which will turn out to be only a contraction if seen within the weekly time frame.

So, "fractal nature" means that what seems to be a well-defined movement, with a change of time frame can appear as something else.

How was the turbulence triggered?

The turbulence (which we saw as a kind of contraction but wider if seen within the daily time frame, a mixture of contraction and expansion) is triggered by two impulses in opposite directions.

So, the turbulence is triggered by a last expansive impulse which is followed by another expansive impulse in the opposite direction.

WHAT IS THE POINT OF ANALYZING VOLATILITY?

Analyzing volatility is useful to adjust one's operations.

In moments of expansion, trend-following strategies and indicators work.

These strategies are based on the price movement, which is exasperated during the expansion.

In moments of contraction, the so-called "mean reversals" work.

These oscillating strategies are based on price equilibrium.

**The longer a contraction phase lasts,
the stronger the following expansion phase will be.**

So, if we have a very long squeezing, maybe on more time frames, and we see that the Bollinger Bands are narrowing, it means that the following expansion will be impulsive.

This leads to an opportunity: by making an anticipatory entry, in fact, we face a nice Trend and therefore the profit greatly exceeds the possible risk.

If the market is in phase of turbulence, it is better to let it cool down.

A good piece of advice is to avoid opening positions during a moment of turbulence, since it is the final part of the trend.

**If a trend is already active and very strong (wide BBWs),
it is not the right moment to plan an entry.**

With very wide Bollinger Bands and also a very high volatility, it is not the time to plan an entry, precisely because it is much more likely that we are close to another compression phase or, even worse, to a terminal phase of the trend itself.

However, if we arrive when the Trend (or the movement) is already fully triggered, it is much better to wait for a more studied entry rather than diving in and risking the decline of the trend.

Beginning of volatility: plan entry on the first tracking

When there are symptoms of the beginning of a trend, it is better to check the sub-time frame and plan an entry.

The stop loss cannot disregard the volatility.

A wider stop loss must be associated to a more volatile market.

On the contrary, if the market is in contraction, doing range trading we must use a narrower stop loss.

The average true range is very useful in case of automatic Trading Systems.

Extreme contraction = unpredictable turbulences

In the phases of strong squeezing (i.e., when the BBW is low on more time frames) it is necessary to take into account that the exit (even if fake) from the range will cause unpredictable turbulences and even trigger the stop loss unintentionally.

Therefore, it is better to wait and avoid opening positions.

FOOD FOR THOUGHT

- **It may be interesting to do a Heatmap of the BBW.**

This means finding the hot zone, the warm zone and the cold zone in the BBW to try to understand in which phase we are.

Each time frame will have its own Heatmap because the values can be very different from each other.

- **Making the BBs on the BBWs**

What does it mean?

It means applying the Bollinger Bands on the Bollinger Bands Width to identify the breaks: the moments when the Bollinger Bands Width goes out of its standard deviation. This is interesting because BBWs are often trigger moments.

- **Watching BBW peaks**

It can be useful to observe the peaks of the Bollinger Bands Width in volatile phases for 2 reasons:

- If they are rising peaks, it means that the excitement always increasing at each movement is a very participated trend.
- On the other hand, if there are more flattened peaks (similar to hollows), they often indicate phases of turbulence and chaos.

This is due to the fact that usually the apical phases of volatility must last a short time.

If they start to last a long time, it means that there is chaos.

Therefore, also a permanence in a warm zone of the Heatmap must never be excessive, otherwise it could exasperate the Trend in progress and become risky.

Example on the chart:

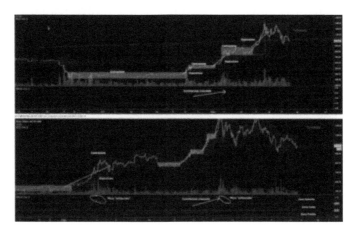

Here we have two examples on the Daily time frame (top chart) and the 4-hour time frame (bottom chart).

Let's start with the Daily: we have our repeating contraction-expansion cycle, and this peak is lower than the next one.

So, we have a very strong trend in progress.

The baseline remains higher because the excitement is so widespread that even the contraction phases are never still.

Like a straw fire ready to catch fire.

In the 4-hour trend (that is a bit more eloquent) we have an example of Heatmap:

Below 0.10 cold zone

Between 0.10 and 0.20 warm zone

Above 0.20 hot zone

In the first peak we can observe more permanence in the hot zone, which means turbulence risk.

The resulting flattened peak was also an anomaly, but it makes us understand that there is a lot of excitement, so there is a lot of turbulence.

When these situations occur, I personally prefer to take a step back because it is difficult to plan positions.

In fact, there are Bart movements and turbulences, so I prefer to play it safe and avoid unnecessary disproportionate risks.

In the second turbulence (marked in yellow) we find increasing excitement, increasing highs and lows on volatility, and another flattened peak: the beginning of the turbulent phase.

Therefore, we had three peaks in the hot zone, one after the other, quickly and abruptly, and this makes us understand that it is really difficult to manage such a situation.

STOP LOSS: WHAT IT IS AND HOW TO USE IT

In this chapter, we will talk about stop loss.

The stop loss is the type of order that allows us to cut losses (as the name implies) and, therefore, makes us understand when to close the position at a loss.

The stop loss is the backbone of any trading strategy as it allows us first of all to limit the losses and also to understand how much to risk or better, how much the market must move to make us lose what we have risked.

On the basis of it, we will also build the possible profit, evaluate the convenience of a position and above all we will be able to evaluate the performance over time.

In this chapter we will face different aspects related to the stop loss starting obviously from what it is, how to use it, how to manage it according to the type of position, how to establish the stop loss in long term positions (maybe even in holding) etc.

STOP LOSS: INSTRUCTIONS FOR USE

The stop loss allows you to cut one of the few things in Trading that can be controlled: losses.

And on the controllable things it is necessary to build strategies.

Therefore, you should start from the parameters that can be managed, manage them in an intelligent way and develop a strategy that can be profitable over time.

WHAT IS THE STOP LOSS?

Let's start by simply saying that the stop loss is a type of order, the stop order, that must be activated when the market refutes the scenario or the set up on which we have operated, closing the position at a loss.

There are different methods of stop loss positioning.

The most classic one is to set it in such a way that when the market reaches a price that is opposite to the market movement on which our position is based, we take the loss and close the position.

Depending on the position, long or short, the stop loss will be:

Stop Sell: long position (purchase), we will have to sell at a loss;

Stop Buy: short position (sale), with a negative profit we have a loss.

It is always better to use a Market Order as stop loss to be sure of its execution.

This is because, if the limit price is slightly different from the stop price, in case of a very strong Dump there is the risk that the stop limit is not executed.

It is convenient to set the limit price in such a way that (being based on the market) it overlaps with the Order Book traits.

THERE IS NO TRADE WITHOUT STOP LOSS

Since there is no certainty about the future, it is necessary to be ready to allow for the error: STOP LOSS

When we hypothesize a position and open it, we must already know in which case that position is wrong.

For example, opening a long position, we must already have in mind how much the price must fall to make us understand that we have failed.

A trade without a stop loss is an unplanned trade

If we don't establish a stop loss, our entire strategy could be blown.

The concept of capital at risk could be invalidated.

We need to know how much we are willing to lose (to risk) for that position, otherwise it will become impossible to calculate the Risk to Reward ratio (R/R) and we will not even know how much, depending on the capital risked, we could earn if the trade goes into profit.

The lack of stop loss inexorably leads to one of these cases:

- **A strong drawdown:** if we put in all our capital and there is a downtrend, we will see our capital dry up.
- **Minimize profit:** not setting a stop loss is equivalent to putting in zero.
- **It will not be assessable**

In non-speculative trades (accumulation, long-term, etc.) there must be a condition of close at a loss.

This is something we will focus on a lot during this chapter, because there are so many clichés that can hijack the correct thinking and perception of the position.

In short: trading and lack of stop loss are two things that cannot coexist!

DIFFERENT TYPES OF STOP LOSS

Classic stop loss: closing a position at a loss if the price falls below a certain threshold.

Stop loss post candle close: closing the position at a loss only if a candle of a specific time frame falls below the predefined price.

- Pros: it protects against sudden impulses (stop hunters);
- Cons: the capital at risk can vary significantly (risk of sudden dumps).

Trailing Stop: moving stop loss.

It can be changed according to the evolution of our position, without ever lowering it from the minimum starting SL.

In this way if the price rises, we can follow the trend by changing the stop loss (below new lows for short positions and above new highs for long)

- Pros: position (and profit) optimization.
- Cons: it requires active management of the position, the stop loss must be checked periodically and set manually.

STOP LOSS AND LONG-TERM POSITIONS (Long-term, Accumulation and Holding)

Now that we know what the various types of stop loss are, let's try to understand how to set them in long-term positions.

In the case of speculative positions, it is mandatory to set the stop loss using longer time frames.

For long-term open positions, we can use weekly or monthly time frames to define the stop loss. In case of "amateur" positions, take into account that:

- Deciding not to define any stop loss means being ready to lose everything:

Capital at risk=100% R/R= 1 if the asset makes X2

- Being willing to lose X%= setting the stop loss at -X% is a valid idea, only if you do not change the percentage during the position.
- "I buy and then see what happens in X years" is equivalent to not setting the SL, because anything could happen from now to X years.

TRADING OR HOLDING

Hence the classic question:

Trading or holding?

What should we do?

What would we like to do?

What it is convenient for us to do?

Does it make sense to do Holding in some situations and Trading in others?

It depends on one's objectives, capital, portfolio and on an infinite number of factors that we will not deal with in this chapter.

It is not possible to start trading and, after realizing that we are not able to do it, switch to holding and leave the trading positions open.

Let's start with very clear ideas without falling into cognitive dissonance.

Holding

Holding is the execution of a single position with:

- Stop loss at zero;
- Entry price at the average purchase price (it would be wise to do cost averaging);
- Size equal to the capital at risk (for example, if we open a $1000 position, the capital at risk will be $1000, because the SL is at zero);
- Take profit unknown

Also in the case of holding, it is necessary to have an exit policy (e.g., imposing ourselves to invest/hold the capital for 5 years).

Certainly, it does not make sense to evaluate it on the basis of the Trading parameters, because (as you have seen in the points listed above) we cannot know the take profit a priori, the capital at risk is total, the Risk to Reward ratio is very low and, therefore, the only cases of real gain in holding are extreme cases (for example when the asset makes x100 or x1000).

Holding is based on the assumption of appreciation of the asset over time.

Holders are not only those who want to bet on x1000.

For example, opening a 1 million position, if the market makes +10% we will earn $100,000, which is not a bad sum, but we also expose ourselves to a considerable risk of loss.

The risk and the potential profit, in this case, always go hand in hand.

Holding is less stressful than trading but has less potential.

Opening a single position, holding implies less stress but has objectively less potential, because, being a single position, it doesn't exploit the Trends and the recession phases, we can't do hedging, etc.

Obviously, it is not to be demonized, but it is not the only way.

You have to understand what you want and manage it accordingly.

THINKING PROCESS OF THE STOP LOSS POSITIONING

1. **Setup definition:**

Why are we opening the position?

What setup are we using? (e.g., Breakout retest? Anticipatory setup?)

1. **Stop Loss Definition:**

What price does the market need to reach in order to invalidate our position?

(For example, if we are opting for a Breakout retest, we could set the stop loss just before the breakout)

1. **Definition of Take Profit:**

Once the profit target is defined, we need to ask ourselves:

How far are the take profit and stop loss from the entry?

At this point we need to calculate the Risk to Reward Ratio.

1. **Evaluation:**

Is it worth opening a position with these parameters?

Is the R/R good? Is the stop loss too wide/narrow?

Once we have all the data at our disposal, we can evaluate whether to make a possible recalculation, changing for example time frame or stop loss, or we can decide to abandon the position and not open it.

TRICKS FOR THE STOP LOSS POSITIONING

Pay attention to stop hunting!

Avoid placing the stop loss on obvious areas corresponding to supports and resistances or just above or below them.

In the previous chart, for example, I have left a little space between the price on which I calculate the stop loss and the actual stop loss to protect myself from stop hunting, even if this also widens the stop loss.

We have to find some middle ground.

We can fragment the stop loss in more orders.

We can place the stop loss on two different levels, in order to mediate the loss exit. By doing this, however, we will have to change the calculation of the capital at risk.

If there are candles with very long shadows nearby, always define the stop loss beyond the shadows themselves.

In the previous chart, you can see that I have positioned the stop loss beyond the shadows but not above the close, to avoid the risk of stop hunting.

In this case the order book is scarcely populated, there is little liquidity and it is easy for the price to touch the stop loss.

The more the time frame is reduced, the more distance should be left between the effective price and the stop loss.

If we use a reduced time frame (for example 1, 2 or 4 hours) the distance must increase a little bit to avoid the stop loss.

HOW TO BALANCE A PORTFOLIO: HEDGING AND DIVERSIFICATION

We have reached the last chapter of the first part of this book.

In this chapter we will talk about Diversification, Exposure and Hedging, which are advanced concepts but fundamental to understand in order to be able to weigh one's own portfolio in a dynamic way.

We will learn how to modify it over time, on different assets, on different strategies and on different time frames, in order to reduce the catastrophic scenarios as much as possible.

DIVERSIFICATION, EXPOSURE AND HEDGING

In this chapter we will deal with themes which are extremely useful for the management of one's own portfolio, with the aim of reducing in particular the Drawdown risk.

For those who do not remember, drawdown is the situation in which our entire portfolio loses value.

It must be avoided because we must not expose ourselves in such a way as to allow the market to bring down our capital, our Equity in a short time (perhaps with a single impulsive move).

To do this there are techniques based in particular on diversification and Hedging, which are two extremely related things.

Optimal subdivision of the portfolio to optimize the risk

The subdivision of the portfolio will be dynamic and not static.

This is because markets change, so we have to change our asset allocation in the portfolio.

The ultimate goal is to optimize the risk.

I used the term "optimize" and not "minimize," because with a higher level of risk there is a higher potential, and therefore, sometimes it is not a despicable situation.

DIVERSIFY: AN ALWAYS RIGHT MANTRA?

We will start with diversification because that's what the other two concepts are based on.

Generally speaking, diversifying is extremely sensible and rational, because investing all your capital in a single asset is unwise.

A capital must always be invested in several assets.

Let's imagine having all our capital invested in Bitcoin, a market (as we know) extremely volatile, that in one day can surprise us with -10%.

By doing this, we expose ourselves to a particularly marked drawdown.

Not a good situation!

So, it is good to invest your capital in more than one asset.

Even better if they are assets belonging to different categories which are not related to each other.

The ideal is to minimize the correlation of the assets we have in our portfolio.

Of course, for those of us who are primarily interested in cryptos, this means ranging outside of cryptos, because actually having an investment portfolio that only includes cryptos exposes you to an exaggeratedly high risk.

Choosing which assets to include in your portfolio and what weight to give to each.

For example, in terms of percentage, we might have a certain number of "A" assets, another number of "B" assets, and a total of "C" assets.

Based on what do we choose the assets?

- Availability of capital in relation to the price of the asset and its return

(Example: if we have $5,000, we will not invest them in real estate);

- Risk appetite:

If we have a bigger capital, perhaps we will be less inclined to risk it and we will want an investment with a lower return, with less risk.

In fact, even a smaller return on a large capital is still satisfying.

On the contrary, if we have a small capital, maybe we will overexpose ourselves a little to risk because we are more willing to reduce it (because in terms of percentage it is a smaller reduction), but we aim to have a more marked profit to increase this capital.

- Situation of the relative markets: it is necessary to observe the performance of the markets of the assets we are buying, looking only at the Primary Trends (long-term macro trends) and keeping the indices, which give us an overview of the market trend itself.

Diversify. Yes, but wisely.

It is useless to diversify by buying assets from a category whose market is falling.

Sometimes it is better to limit the range of assets and maybe concentrate on 2/4 markets rather than over-fragmenting and losing sight of the overall situation.

RISK OF CERTAIN ASSETS

Let's deepen the discussion on risk.

Diversification, by necessity, cannot focus on just one type of asset.

It is not right to operate 100% on one asset because there is a whole range of other assets that could balance our portfolio.

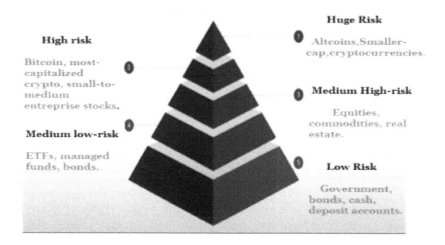

At the top of the pyramid, you can see the higher risk assets, because a balanced portfolio has obviously a higher percentage invested in low-risk assets and a lower percentage as the risk increases.

We will examine the pyramid starting from the bottom:

Low Risk:

Government securities, Liquidity, Bank deposit accounts

Medium-Low Risk:

ETFs, Managed Funds, Bonds

Medium-High Risk:

Equities, Commodities, Real Estate

High risk:

Bitcoin, most-capitalized Cryptos, small or mid-cap Stocks

Disproportionate risk:

Altcoins, small-cap Cryptocurrencies

If we realize that commodities are in a strong up-trend and Bitcoin is in a downtrend, we could "re-weigh" our positions and reduce our investment on Bitcoin in favor of commodities.

We need to be dynamic and follow up-trends as well because that is how we can profit.

Obviously rebalancing the assets does not mean selling all the Bitcoins and moving all our capital on commodities!

We should check our portfolio and the primary trends on a daily or weekly basis and (even without going crazy on the charts) rebalance our positions accordingly.

RISK AND PARAMETERS

After having analyzed the risk of some assets, let's see what influences us in the choice of the risk to which we expose ourselves.

What is it that predisposes us more or less to risk?

Higher income

The less money we need, the greater risk appetite we can afford.

We can risk more our invested capital since we can still maintain a good standard of living with our income.

Lower invested capital

It makes little sense to invest a small capital in low-risk assets because we will get a low return.

For example, if we have $5000, we will not buy government bonds, because we would earn practically nothing. It is a very low percentage (1-2% per year).

Younger age

An investor at a younger age can bear a greater risk, because s/he has a longer time horizon.

On the contrary, a person close to retirement age will try to preserve more his/her capital, rather than risk it to increase it.

OTHER DIVERSIFICATION METHODS

Splitting positions among different assets is not the only method of diversification.

There are several methods which can be more or less speculative.

By speculation I mean the short-term operation that, in my opinion, fits very well with the long-term operation in order to further diversify.

Now let's divide again operation in different branches, which will help us spread more our portfolio without having to look after too many assets, that is working on the same asset by dividing operation in several sections.

Time frame diversification

Long-term trading carries less risk.

On the contrary, more aggressive trading (with a lower time frame) carries more risk. Combining these two things could decrease our risk.

Obviously, the capital on a low time frame (LTF) should always be very limited to avoid drawdown risk.

Strategic diversification

By allocating capital to trades based on different setups, we mitigate our overall risk slightly, while remaining tied to the risk of the assets we are exposed to.

In this way we divide our operation, even if we are dealing with the same asset, on different strategies.

For example, we can open a long-term position on Bitcoin with a part of capital still to ride the primary trend, a second part of capital based on a specific position (a Breakout, for example, to enjoy that impulse) and a third part of capital on a range aimed at maximizing the return during that specific range.

By crossing together, they mitigate each other.

Hedging diversification

Hedging is a mixed operation which allows us to defend ourselves against market movements that put us at risk of high drawdown.

We must have a plan B ready and already active that can protect us from that situation.

THE CONCEPT OF EXPOSURE

To explore the theme of hedging we must first introduce the concept of exposure, as hedging mitigates exposure.

Exposure:

We calculate our exposure to risk on each category of diversification we introduced earlier (on an asset, a category, a time frame, a strategy, etc.).

It is related to the percentage of capital allocated on positions in the same direction on correlated assets.

Exposure can be measured in 2 ways:

- Based on multiples of R: capital at risk on open positions (calculated on "base currency");

- For positions without stop loss, the exposure is measured as a percentage of the total capital of that dedicated fraction of the portfolio.

Example:
Equity: $10,000 R=2%.
Opening of the following positions:
Long on Bitcoin X2R
Long on ETH for XR
Short on XRP XR/2
Buy&Hold BTC for $15,000
Exposures:
15% on BTC, and of the remaining 85,000 (R calculated on them)
+2R on BTC
+R on ETH
-R/2 on XRP

To evaluate if we are over or underexposed, we should compare the risk of each asset, and then on the basis of the parameters that we have defined we will determine if we are within the terms.

For example, we may decide not to expose ourselves more than 30% overall on Bitcoin.

In this case we would have 15%+4% (2R), +2% (1R), +1% (R/2) = 22%.

The exposure is correct according to our parameters.

It is important to give yourself canons in order to learn from the past and their evolution over time, understanding how your portfolio, your emotions and risk appetite react and how comfortable you feel in that situation, rebalancing your thresholds if you risk being too exposed.

THE CONCEPT OF HEDGING

Finally, we have the concept of HEDGING: a favorable combination of several positions whose outcome is inversely correlated.

That means trying to balance one's exposure by perhaps adding a negative exposure as opposed to a positive one.

Hedging on a single asset:

By opening a short position and a long one, by playing well with entry and stop loss, we will benefit from both outcomes.

Example: we can open a long with a stop loss close enough to the low range and open a short on the high range, with a stop loss above the high range.

Wherever this position will break, we will enjoy some profit.

The exposure is therefore differentiated between two similar and opposite positions.

Hedging A/B/C:

Exposure on 3 assets: A, B and C.

If the A/B positions are in a downtrend but A/C and B/C are in a correlated uptrend, we can go LONG on A/C and SHORT on B/C, obtaining an unbalanced "leverage effect" in our favor.

Example: A= BTC B=ETH C=$

A/B (BTC/ETH) is in downtrend, while C ($) is in uptrend.

A/C (BTC/$) we go LONG; it is so much in uptrend that it causes B/C to uptrend.

B/C (ETH/$) we go SHORT.

In this way, if there is a bullish continuation, our LONG on A/C will be much stronger than the losses suffered by the SHORT on B/C.

If the trend becomes bearish given the downtrend of A/B, the short on B/C will yield much more than the stop loss that the LONG gives us on A/C.

This is a synthetic leverage effect, unbalanced in our favor.

Multi Time Frame Hedging:

It means combining a position on the primary trend (HTF: High Time Frame) with a reverse position on a minor trend (LTF: Low Time Frame).

Example chart:

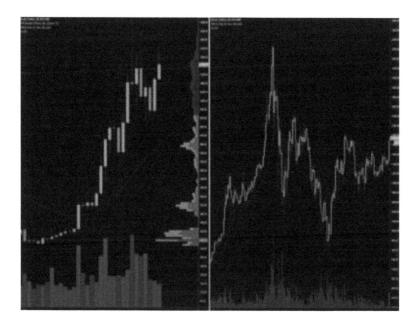

Look at the Bitcoin chart seen in two different Trends: the first on the weekly time frame and the second on the 2-hour time frame.

Do you see how different it is? Because the peak on the weekly chart is equivalent to the peak on the 2-hour time frame.

Therefore, on the weekly TF, we undoubtedly keep our positions open without blinking an eye, since we have Higher Highs and Higher Lows.

In order to take more advantage of the close situation, we can open a short when we see a Lower High.

We can open a short in Multi Time Hedging, so that we can exploit the countermovement, choosing if we want to put a take profit or even keep the position open to the bitter end.

In this case, maybe if we arrive early, we can take advantage of a potential market reversal to gain from the short.

Also in this situation, by positioning the stop loss in a wise way, we will be able to obtain a R/R that can balance the opposite position in an optimal way.

ASSET ALLOCATION

We have arrived at the second part of this book, which will deal with operation.

We will learn to build a portfolio starting from nothing, to manage a trading system and a Trading Journal and, finally, we will understand how to integrate Trading and Investment with concrete examples.

In this chapter we will talk about Asset Allocation, i.e., how to define the capital you can invest depending on your economic conditions and how to understand the way to invest it.

This will be the foundation to start building a portfolio and a long-term capital management strategy.

CAPITAL ALLOCATION AND INITIAL SETUP

Let's start with asset allocation, which is the first issue to address in operational terms in order to build a solid foundation for your investment strategy.

How much to invest?

What is the risk tolerance?

What are the different risk classes depending on the asset?

How much to expose yourself in terms of monetization?

INVESTMENT OBJECTIVES

Protect the capital from inflation:

By not leaving cash in the account, we avoid losing that 2% annually imposed by inflation (i.e., when prices rise and money loses value).

Get an additional source of income:

Free ourselves from the slavery of salary as our only source of income.

This is often the beginning of a path towards financial independence and education.

Creating or growing a family capital to pass down as an inheritance:

An investment designed to make life easier for those who will come after us by leaving them our wealth accumulated over time.

Create a private retirement fund:

Putting aside something more (in addition to what perhaps the common retirement funds already give) in an obviously very long-term perspective.

This will be added to the income from small investments.

In summary, the purpose of an investment is to grow our capital over time as much as possible by controlling the risk.

Although this sentence seems trivial, it is not!

In fact, we can notice two variables:

- As much as possible.
- Controlling the risk.

The first one, "as much as possible", requires looking for assets that grow in value more than others. However, "controlling the risk" is something that goes against the latter, because the assets with higher growth potential are usually the riskier ones.

So, putting these two things together (risk and return) is always the fundamental equation of investing, and must be exactly our goal.

This can be achieved with several techniques that we will learn and explore in these chapters.

DEFINING INVESTABLE CAPITAL

Let's start with the basics: deciding how much we can afford to invest.

In order to do this, we should keep our feet on the ground, we can't fantasize about crazy investments if we are struggling to make ends meet.

We have to be extremely honest and sincere with ourselves and ask ourselves the question: how much can we afford to invest?

Of course, it is not necessary to do it all at once, we can do it every month, every semester, every trimester (depending on various factors that we will have to evaluate personally by calculating income and expenditure), we can devote a slice of capital to an investment portfolio, make accumulation plans, allocate that capital to the investment portfolio, etc.

So, we will have two different accounts, one of which is the cash account (in the bank) and the other is the investment account, which can be either cash or invested.

Income

- SALARY
- PROPERTY
- MISCELLANEOUS INCOME

Fixed expenses

- TAXES
- BILLS
- RENT
- DEBTS

Variable expenses

- HOLIDAYS
- MAINTENANCE
- CARS
- MEDICAL EXPENSES
- FAMILY EXPENSES

Cash buffer

It is unwise to leave your portfolio empty because variable expenses are not always predictable.

Investable capital

The rest can be allocated as investible capital.

A very simple calculation:

Income -

Fixed expenses -

Variable expenses -

Cushion =

Investment Capital

So, from our income (salary, property and miscellaneous income) we will have to subtract fixed expenses (easily predictable expenses: debts, rent, bills, taxes: everything that comes out periodically) and variable expenses (car maintenance, house maintenance, medical expenses, family expenses, etc.).

In variable expenses we also put holidays because we don't have to stop living a good life to invest everything.

The cash buffer should also be subtracted from the income.

It is a sort of stock, a cash tank, to be kept in the bank account for unforeseen expenses (other variable expenses: car breakdown, medical expenses, etc.).

We must be certain that we can cope with these types of emergencies, the investment must not take away our security, we must be able to afford it.

All that remains after subtracting the various expenses is the investible capital.

From this calculation we can already understand that in the event of an emergency, what we can act on is variable expenses and income, i.e., we can work more or spend less to have more capital.

I strongly advise against investing when we cannot afford it, because otherwise we risk deducting capital from the cash buffer that we can always use for various contingencies. This is far more important than having investible capital.

Let's rather eliminate unnecessary expenses and try to increase income so that we can invest the surplus.

Our economic framework also affects our risk tolerance

(higher risk=lower tolerance).

If we have more expenses, we will need a somewhat larger cash buffer, we will be forced to invest less and, in this situation, we will be even less willing to risk our capital.

We would like less risk for less potential return and this is obviously a personal thing.

Each person is in a different situation and needs to know how risk-tolerant s/he is according to his/her economic situation and how much s/he can afford to invest.

The important thing is to understand these concepts.

VERY IMPORTANT NOTIONS

The invested capital must not affect your life in any way.

We cannot eat bread and water to reduce variable expenses and have more capital to invest! We must not invest too much and be left without liquidity in our account in the event of unforeseen events (or worse, with debts in fixed expenses!).

Give up unnecessary whims if you want to have more investible capital.

By simply organizing monthly or weekly budgets, we will be able to see where we spend, more or less, and where we could avoid spending.

After that, we will know how much of our portfolio capital to devote to investments. Trust me, it doesn't take much to change your situation over time.

If you are consistent and focus on your goals, you can really achieve great results with little effort.

In a difficult situation we are not in a position to plan an investment.

If you find yourself in a difficult situation (over-indebtedness, difficulty in making ends meet, etc.) you are not in a position to plan an investment.

It is better to work on other aspects of your financial situation, such as income and expenses (finding a further job, looking for a better-paid job, limiting expenses, etc.).

ALLOCATION OF THE CAPITAL TO INVEST

Now that we have understood how much we can invest, let's see where to invest.

Investing in something that can increase in value over time

This can be done by observing the long-term trend (graphical analysis) or with the fundamental analysis.

The trend analysis can refer to the purchase of a stock that at the moment is underpriced or whose company has always good profits and protects the investors.

Otherwise, we can simply look at a chart from above, with monthly or weekly time frame and see an uptrend setting, of which the market is pushing the stock upwards, and then decide to invest.

One thing we can do to understand the current market phase in terms of graphical analysis is to look at stock indices, such as the Ftse Mib, the DAX, the SP 500, the stock trend of a particular country, a particular category, etc.

There are indices for every taste and for every typology and from here, making a basic technical analysis, we can observe the trends: moving averages, Higher Highs, Higher Lows, supports and resistances, etc.

On the other hand, the fundamental analysis refers to the purchase, for example, of a stock, an asset or a property in which we see a growth in value over time for fundamental reasons (for example if the property is located in a city whose real estate value is growing).

Investing to diversify our assets

Clearly it makes no sense to invest everything in a single asset or category.

However, be careful not to over-diversify, because you would struggle to follow your investment and its evolution.

We have to know the asset we are investing in; we have to observe it day after day, read the news, read the company's report if it is a stock.

We have to know whether the terms of fundamental analysis or graphical analysis according to which we entered this investment still apply.

We need to have clear in mind what we are doing and how our investments are doing.

Obviously the better you know your investment, the more you understand it, you know how it moves, its seasonality, and the better your performance will be.

We have to focus on what we know, and if we want to extend our range of investments, we have to study it properly first.

Never jump into something you don't know.

Investing to control risk

This is a type of investment for which we can set up a strategy of quantifying the investment risk (knowing how much we are risking at any given time) and the risk of cutting losses, because the only thing you can control are the losses.

The gain cannot be known, the losses can be limited.

This is what mathematically defines risk and must be used precisely and consistently.

RISK PYRAMIDIZATION

Risk pyramidization is a very simple strategy that you can use to build your portfolio.

Imagine a pyramid with a broad base and a narrow tip:

- The base must be solid and, in this case, represents the portfolio.

First of all, it is advisable to build a more resistant base of low-risk assets, perhaps with returns (such as shares) that historically represent irreplaceable companies, which can only grow over time and which do not know competition (securities, dividends, coupons, etc.).

This is to avoid unbalancing our portfolio.

A portfolio that is too speculative is not safe.

- As these assets mature and we have a solid base with more liquidity, we can go for more speculative investments.

For example, with the return on this low risk first year investments we can buy more speculative investments.

- The portfolio should not be unbalanced towards the tip of the pyramid, but towards the base.

Many people reverse this principle, perhaps they have not too much capital to invest or are in a hurry and risk everything they have.

This is a wrong principle because in this way one risks destroying the capital.

The risk becomes excessive and unmanageable.

Pyramiding risk in this way is a very strong first strategy to contain and control it.

INVESTMENT DIVERSIFICATION

Let's try to better understand some of the asset categories.

INVESTABLE CAPITAL:

- MEDIUM/LOW RISK (PYRAMID BASE)

– Bonds/cash (Liquidity)

– Stocks typical of holders of safe-deposit boxes (Coca Cola, Amazon, etc.)

ETFs (index funds: pharmaceutical sector, etc.)

- MEDIUM/HIGH RISK (PYRAMID TIP)

– Growth stocks/ Small cap/ Commodities/ Speculative assets/ Real estate
– Cryptocurrencies/ P2P lending/ DeFi/ CeFi

INVESTING OR TRADING?

Investing

Investing means allocating capital to assets in which we perceive a higher future value (compared to today, of course).

So, it's like saying "I don't want cash, because cash loses value over time. I want something that grows in value over time."

We don't have a defined time frame, it's an alternative to liquidity.

Trading

Trading, on the contrary, is a speculative operation with a well-defined and limited time frame.

It can be one day, one month, one year, two years... but the aim is to make a profit in a limited time frame.

Investing and trading can work together in the following cases:

- Using trading as a hedge for investment.

For example, if the market is in recession, we can trade short and hedge our investment.

By doing this, we will minimize losses and turn them into profit.

- Enhancer: exploiting trading movements to enhance investments.

In this case, imagine that we have invested in Bitcoin, during uptrends we can speculatively trade long in buying, therefore amplifying our position.

- Stand-alone

A term to describe trading only, avoiding long-term investments.
This, however, is much more difficult and involves higher risks.

LIFE CYCLE OF A POSITION

1. Entry Strategy
2. Management Strategy
3. Exit strategy

The life cycle of any position is the following:

Entry strategy:
Definition of an entry strategy (from dollars to asset).

Management strategy:
Management of the investment ongoing, i.e., everything that happens during the position, e.g., hedging, exposure amplification, trading, partial exits, loss limitation, etc.

Exit strategy:
Exit strategy (from asset to dollars).

We always need to know when to exit (e.g., when the company we invested in starts to perform worse than expected, or if our strategy is to exit the asset during the worst phases of the market, etc.).

We will address these 3 phases individually depending on the various investment or trading strategies in the next chapter.

CHOOSING
THE BEST STRATEGY

In this chapter we will see how to set up a generic investment and trading strategy.

We will do this by starting with an analysis of the personal situation, trying to understand how we can act based on experience, market presence, emotions and many other things.

We will divide experience and ability into different levels to make everything more concrete, and we will see how to progress from one level to the next so that we never stop improving, and then we will be able to use all the different techniques available to operate.

In order to fully understand this chapter, we will need the fundamental concepts of the setup, discussed in the first part, which I suggest you revise.

In the first chapter we understood how to invest the capital (how much to invest, how to allocate it by building a portfolio based on risk criteria, etc.), while in this chapter we will set up an investment strategy for each of these assets.

CHOOSING AND DEFINING STRATEGY AND OPERATION

How to define a strategy and operation for your portfolio.

THE BASICS

Everything is based on experience. If we do not have experience in trading and investing in markets, the first thing to do is to study and gain experience.

Before starting to invest you need to have some basic knowledge:

- Know the market on which you are going to operate;
- Know the asset you are buying;
- Know the platforms on which to operate (Exchanges, Brokers, etc.);
- Know how to manage the asset between purchase and sale... and know how to store it!

If we think about storing metals, we will need to know how long and where to store it or, in the case of assets, we will need to consider its financial aspects.

- now your investible capital (have a defined plan).

CHOOSING STRATEGY AND OPERATION

Choosing operation must depend on experience and market presence, in order of importance we will have:

Trading knowledge:

To be able to choose a strategy, it is necessary to know the basics of investing and trading (Holding, Higher Frequency Trading, etc.)

Trading experience:

Trading is a very complicated activity that needs to be learned a little at a time and then assimilated over time.

Emotional profile:

Our psychological side plays an important role in trading and, unfortunately, we don't realize this until we get involved.

Fear, emotions and impulsiveness can take over (Bias).

This often clouds our mind a lot because it tends to create expectations on Trading which are always higher than reality.

We need to know ourselves and be realistic with ourselves.

Time available to devote to following, analyzing markets and operating

The market presence is fundamental to adapt one's strategy.

Knowledge of derivative and speculative instruments

Not knowing the derivative and speculative instruments does not absolutely prevent us from trading, but it does preclude some possibilities, for example Hedging, Futures, Options, Perpetuals, etc.

They allow us to operate even more aggressively and include other variables.

The more instruments we know, the more we can combine them to create more complex strategies and have more possibilities in different situations.

WHAT DOES IT MEAN TO GAIN EXPERIENCE? HOW DOES ONE GAIN EXPERIENCE?

I have defined four types of operation based on experience in Trading:

1. No trading knowledge → Accumulation Plan (Holding)

For those who have no Trading knowledge whatsoever, I recommend avoiding Trading!

Better to start learning little by little and start investing with a simple accumulation plan.

You can start with periodic purchases and sales, without following the market, on assets in which you see potential and appreciation.

Study an active entry strategy and an active exit strategy, following the results of your accumulation plan over time.

Example: let's consider Bitcoin. We are aware that in the next 10 years it will be worth more, so we set up an accumulation plan with fraction of capital allocated to Bitcoins.

1. Little trading experience → Trend Follower HTF operation

If you are inexperienced, it is better to use a High Time Frame (HTF).

In particular, following a weekly or monthly time frame requires less market presence and there are fewer fluctuations in the charts.

The trend follower operation allows us to rely on market trends, with purchases and sales influenced by signals of trend start and end (also called swing trading).

1. Good trading experience → Mixed HTF+LTF operation

In this hypothetical level 3 you can combine several time frames, creating two different types of operation:

- Trend follower (as in level 2)
- Operation based on setups with particular Price Action oriented settings: look at the chart, identify the setup and open a short-term position.

These setups are based on a technique of risk limitation and return calculation (R/R) and are to be included in a trading system, which is a subject we will address in the next chapters.

1. **Maximum trading experience → Mixed trading + Hedges with derivatives**

A person with the highest level of experience will be able to deal with mixed operation (LTF+HTF), as in level 3, but with the addition of hedges and derivatives (options, leverages, futures, etc.).

This type of operation can amplify positions or cushion losses.

HOW TO GAIN TRADING EXPERIENCE

So how do we progress through these 4 levels?

By trying!

We have understood that studying is fundamental: following the assets, understanding how the market works, observing charts day after day, etc.

However, it is not passive observation that will lead us to success, but some of the following factors.

Theory alone is useless.

We can read all the books we want, take all the courses we want, watch all the videos we want and we will be great... in theory!

If we don't put that theory into practice, we still know nothing about trading.

Simulated trading.

This is a useful tool only for learning how to use the platforms.

In fact, trading with demo accounts is of extremely limited use because it completely excludes the emotional part.

On these platforms the money is not real, it is not ours and therefore we will never feel the same sensations as when we put our real capital at risk.

Therefore, in the reality we won't replicate the same results as in the tests; they are not comparable in the slightest.

We need real capital to include the emotional component, which is the most influential one.

There is a gulf between those who are good at making analysis and those who are good at trading.

We can be very good at analyzing diagrams, drawing rows, observing the Trends, but defining when to enter, with how much capital to enter, when to exit and where to put the stop loss is all another thing.

Low capital to limit losses.

The beginning will be at a loss, we have to keep it in mind.

For this reason, we shouldn't begin with high capital.

Even if the first trades go well, it is always better to remain humble.

The first footsteps will be like a "Trial-and-error game", we will need to try, to make mistakes, to understand where we make mistakes, to modify our approach, to understand our limits and to define a strategy within these limits.

Gradually increase the capital allocated to trading as you gain experience.

We can overcome our initial limits by gaining experience.

By studying a more advanced operation, we can gradually allocate a small percentage of capital to the next level.

The more experience we have, the more we will increase that percentage, until we reach our original plan.

BASIC OPERATION - ACCUMULATION PLAN

Let's try to understand how these strategies are structured.

Let's assume that we want to open an asset for long-term appreciation:

ENTRY STRATEGY:

- Time: within each fixed time frame.
- Performance: evaluating how the asset is performing and what expectations we have on the basis of the analyses.
- Availability: capital defined during the allocation.

MANAGEMENT STRATEGY:

We need to periodically recalculate entry and exit fees (see chapter on accumulation plans).

EXIT STRATEGY:

Exit based on time, performance and availability.

- Time: periodic exit, to avoid losing capital if the trend reverses.
- Performance: assessing how the asset is performing and what expectations we have on the basis of the analyses, taking advantage of the uptrend.
- Availability: capital defined during the allocation.

In short, we enter with a shorter entry time, manage the entries according to how the investment is going, and finally exit periodically to make the most of the uptrend in the long run.

INTERMEDIATE OPERATION - SWING TRADING

Intermediate operation, or swing trading, consists in riding High Time Frame Trends (long term).

The default capital is in Cash (neutral, not invested), the operation involves an entry based on a setup or a trading system that analyzes the Trend.

ENTRY STRATEGY:

Entry based on a setup or trading system that analyses the trend.

In order to do this, we must identify the conditions which are triggering a trend, that can be a setup (for example the breakup of a very important resistance on a weekly time frame, that we expect will generate a trend) or a Trading system (such as the configuration of moving averages, higher highs and higher lows, etc.).

In short, all the conditions that define a trend with good probability to subsist for a while.

MANAGEMENT STRATEGY:

Assessment based on exposure.

The Management strategy evaluates, on the basis of all the parameters of our exposure, how long to remain in, when to exit, whether to make partial take profits and whatever else.

Obviously, these parameters will have to be defined in advance.

During asset allocation we will decide how long to remain exposed in a certain strategy, how long to remain exposed in a certain asset, etc.

There could be big gains or maybe we will begin to capitalize just to hold that exposure we planned at the beginning.

EXIT STRATEGY:

Exit based on invalidation of entry conditions.

The exit strategy occurs when the entry conditions are invalidated.

For example, the end of a Trend implies the stop, the closing of the position.

ADVANCED OPERATION - TRADING

Advanced operation is a higher frequency trading with a default capital in cash and a mixed operation on both Trends and short setups, based on risk and return.

ENTRY STRATEGY:

Entry based on setups or trading systems that analyze the trend and other conditions.

Risk calculation.

The entry strategy is divided in two: one part based on the Trend (identifying trends) and the other based on short setups (based on a risk/return profile).

Therefore, we will check when the chart suggests a certain setup (calculating the risk value and the potential return) and, based on the profitability history of that setup, we will decide whether to enter or not in that position.

MANAGEMENT STRATEGY:

Evaluation based on the exposure and position parameters.

The management strategy will depend on the parameters of exposures and positions (How much are we exposing ourselves on a certain asset? How much have we planned to allocate to it?).

EXIT STRATEGY

Exit based on invalidation of entry conditions (end of trend, Stop loss, Take profit).

PRO OPERATION - TRADING + HEDGING

Default capital in cash.

Mixed operation on trends and R/R setups, with hedging positions.

In this case, in the total exposure we will have:

- Trend follower exposure (swing trading);
- Exposure of setups complementary to it;
- Mitigating the exposure (or amplifying it further) with hedging positions, i.e. using derivative products.

For example, we buy Bitcoins because we notice a medium-term trend, if we are exposed to Long trend followers, but in the short term we notice setups that could undermine that Trend triggering a bearish phase.

Then we can hedge with a short using for example a future.

In this way we reduce our overall exposure and consequently the overall risk of this part of the portfolio.

ENTRY STRATEGY:

Entry based on setups or trading systems that analyze the trend and other conditions.

Risk and exposure calculation.

Compared to advanced operation, exposure is added because hedging is designed to modify exposure.

MANAGEMENT STRATEGY:

Assessment based on exposure and position parameters.

Further assessment of hedging with synthetic leverage.

Synthetic leverage can be obtained by placing very tight stop losses; for the same amount of capital risked, we can obtain a fake leverage effect.

Obviously, the return risk will be much higher even if we increase the position risk.

EXIT STRATEGY:

Exit based on invalidation of the entry conditions in the short positions (end of trend, Stop loss, Take profit) or achievement of a level of satisfying total exposure, that allow us to close the hedging positions.

For example, back to the previous case, if the downtrend turns out to be only in the short term, perhaps we make Take profit of that hedging short and we remain exposed like before with the Trend follower system only on HTF.

So, this was a deliberately generic overview, just to make you understand the possible settings of these four strategy levels, ranging from the simple accumulation plan to the more complicated high frequency Trading with hedging positions in derivatives.

CONCLUSIONS

More advanced operation gives you a greater chance of profit, but also more risk.

Certainly, the more positions you open, the more risk of making mistakes and losing there is.

My advice is always the same one: if you have little experience, it's better to open as few positions as possible and stick to the long term.

Gradually approach the advanced difficulties and make the upgrade only once if you are sure of the results on a sufficient time frame.

It is important, before jumping to the next level, not to be in a hurry and not to overestimate yourself (even if it is instinctive), but to wait until you have sufficient results.

Every trading system must undergo a prolonged test period to measure its efficiency.

You will need to draft a Trading Journal, where to include all the operations and estimate objectively the results (we will speak about this in detail in the next chapters).

TRADING SYSTEM

Here we come to the highlight of the second part of this book, dedicated to trading operation.

This will be the richest chapter because we will see what a trading system is, how to recruit it, how to make it work and how to evaluate its performance or possible exclusion.

We have to put ourselves in the shoes of an entrepreneur whose employees are these trading systems, these trading strategies.

We need to have well-defined criteria to hire them, know how to make them work, evaluate their performance while they are working and, if necessary, limit the damage they do if they work badly!

In case they work worse and worse, we should consider firing them, excluding them from the business.

In the meantime, we will explore and do Research & Development to recruit other trading systems which can work in parallel.

Basically, in this chapter dedicated to operation we will see:

- The four phases of a trading system: from planning to putting it into production and evaluating it.
- The analysis of wins and losses, aimed at optimizing the performance of the strategy system over time and making it as spendable as possible.

CREATING AND MAINTAINING A TRADING SYSTEM

The trading system is all about the trading strategy we use and our approach to the market complete with all the details (how to enter, how to exit, how to manage risk, etc.).

We will learn how to create, define and evaluate a trading strategy, dealing with several points:

- Planning
- Testing
- Putting it into production
- Possible modifications (Feedback Loop)

RECRUITING A TRADING SYSTEM

The trading system is a strategy to be implemented on the Market, complete with all the details.

Nothing should be left to chance or discretion, especially at the beginning.

The four phases of recruitment:

- Planning:

Choosing the criteria and strategy to recruit the trading system.

- Backtesting:

Using the recruited trading system on historical data to pre-test its efficiency.

- Testing:

Using the TS in real time, with extremely reduced capital (10% of that used in production).

- Putting into Production:

Gradually increasing the capital at risk, e.g., 1/10 every week of congruent results.

Now we will see each of these phases in detail.

PLANNING PHASE

During this initial phase we need to plan a complete trading strategy, according to these principles:

Reference Time Horizon:

We need to know whether it is a short-term or long-term strategy, whether it is an accumulation plan, Swing Trading or High Frequency Trading.

Allocated Capital:

If it is a long-term strategy, we will talk about allocated capital.

This strategy is closer to investing than to Trading and therefore we will lock a capital on it, the executed trades will be much fewer and the logic will be slightly different.

Allocated risk:

If it is a short-term strategy, we will talk about allocated risk.

If we are operating in the short term, probability will weigh much more heavily, as the number of trades executed increases and probability statistics begin to play a major role. For this reason, it is better to think in terms of allocated risk rather than allocated capital.

Each position must risk a specific amount, which must have been written down.

The rules must be followed.

Setup or Entry and Exit Conditions:

This is the so-called Entry Placement (seen in the previous chapter).

We need to know within what time frame certain specific setups occur (trend followers, breakout strategies and resistances, etc.).

We need to have clear ideas.

Once we know which setups to use and which approach to use, we will be able to evaluate their efficiency, but knowing that we have followed the rules of our setups.

Logically, when it comes to setups or conditions, the type of trading system will depend on the temporal horizon (for example, if it is an accumulation plan, we will not speak of setup, high frequency Trading, risk/return or allocated risk).

Context

Evaluation of the type of context in which to apply the trading system:

Is it a strategy that works during ranging periods?

Is it a strategy that works during trending periods?

Is it a strategy that works when we are in Bull Market?

Bitcoins or Altcoins?

Drawdown management:

The drawdown, as we saw earlier, indicates the maximum loss on our capital. We have to be able to manage these situations (series of losses) and calculate the drawdown not only for the whole portfolio but also for the single trading system.

Let's imagine our portfolio as our business, and the single trading system as an employee that operates according to the instructions that are given to him/her.

The drawdown of the individual employee, of the individual trading system, is very important because it must follow certain instructions too.

We will have to concentrate on the series of losses in order to regularize the drawdown as much as possible.

Eventual hedges

If we want to implement also hedges, we must not forget that it will be a strategy with a maximum level of difficulty and it must be included within the respective setups; for example, during a trend follower in the short term with mixed time frame, we can use a short hedge if we notice some signs of reversal.

Or if we see a range on a daily time frame, during an Uptrend on weekly time frames of course, our strategy will involve a long-term exposure, plus opening a short when this range in the short term is broken downwards.

So, having predefined this setup, when we see the daily downward breakdown with retest of the old support turned into resistance, we will open the hedging position; it is a setup and we need to keep track of it.

Defining "riskiness"

Riskiness means understanding how aggressive our trading system is: if it is a trading system that operates on 5-minute time frames, it will be very risky by nature because it is very aggressive.

We will realize the level of riskiness according to some parameters like setups that operate in anticipated way, very low time frames, high leverages, very high R/R, etc.

BACKTESTING PHASE

Testing the trading system on historical data:

- Context:

In order to create a proper test, we need to identify with the context in which the trading system would be triggered.

If it is a mixed context, which is good in ranges, Bull Market and Bear Market, we should try to test it in all possible market conditions.

If we manage to test it only in a phase, it is convenient at the beginning to apply it only in that phase.

In any case it is necessary to identify with the context in which the trading system is then put into production.

- Committed capital:

During the backtesting phase, we will not have ANY committed capital, as it is a test based on historical data.

This is not a good thing, because the test will not be reliable or trustworthy.

It serves only to understand if the trading system is profitable or not, based on the setups and its entry and exit conditions in the history.

Nevertheless, the "unreliability" factor depends especially on the emotional component, which is completely lacking.

Without capital, we do not activate our emotions and therefore performance is not reliable, we tend to risk more and do things we would not do in production.

Verifying according to evaluation parameters

The backtest remains, in any case, an excellent way to skim, since it verifies the objective result of the setups that the strategy proposes according to evaluation parameters.

If the results are satisfying, we go one step further to the testing phase.

This testing phase will begin to foresee a risked capital by bringing into play the emotional component a little at a time.

Beware of the lack of an emotional component:

- The results obtained during this phase are not reliable at all;
- It is better to simplify Entry and Exit as much as possible, if you have little experience.

For those with less experience, it's advisable to simplify, at least at the beginning.

When we make a backtest, we decide the setup or the entry-exit conditions.

We start with a simple trading system that works, because there are many that work based on market conditions.

There are no rules, there is no right or wrong one.

Find the one that works best for you because emotionality is really predominant.

EVALUATION PARAMETERS

Net profit over a sufficiently large time frame

We should consider a sufficiently large time frame: a minimum of 100 samples for a reliable statistic.

Lowest possible maximum drawdown

We must stick to the lowest possible maximum drawdown, for 2 reasons:

- It is emotionally more bearable.

Enduring a series of losses is the hardest thing ever for a trader.

- More regular equity line.

The equity line is the curve of the performance of our capital allocated to this trading system over time.

It is more regular if the drawdown is cut, smoothing downwards.

Consequently, with a lower drawdown and a more regular equity line, we will have a more expendable and less volatile TS.

Moreover, reducing the volatility of the equity line makes the trading system more spendable over time, more valid and working longer.

We should always take into account that if we reduce the "size" of the position, the profit will diminish too.

Frequency of operations

The frequency of our operations must be compatible with our activities.

For example, if the trading system generates 50 trades a day and we can only look at the charts twice a day, it will not be possible to keep up.

We must therefore set up alerts, stay often in front of the computer with the charts at the ready or use a TS that delivers a frequency of operation setups to be activated, compatible with our activity.

TESTING PHASE

Testing the trading system on the real-time data

Introduction of the emotional component: are we able to manage the TS? How does it make us feel?

The passage from the backtesting phase, based on the history, to the testing phase must occur gradually.

Evaluation and gradual increase of the risked capital

The best option is to divide this process into several steps starting with an initial risk percentage X, increasing it by on step (Z), until we reach nominal risk Y.

The nominal risk, or Y, is 100% and is the capital we have defined in our planning phase for this trading system and for the positions we will open.

We will never start to open positions with the full value of Y, but always with X% of Y.

For example: Y= 100% X=10% of Y Z= % increase

Over time, for each period (one week, one month, two months, etc.) of satisfying results (Net Profit - Maximum Drawdown - Frequency of trades - Emotional Counterparty) that we analyze, we will increase by one step (Z%).

After each step, we have to repeat the test, until we reach 100% (Y), the testing phase ends and the strategy is put into production.

The threshold will seem imperceptible because there is this constant growth of capital or risk committed.

PRODUCTION PHASE

If the previous phases seemed complicated, the production phase is no less so, but we will learn how to manage it with the ongoing changes we need to make. So, now we will look at all the parts which compose the production phase.

DYNAMIC RISK MANAGEMENT

Ongoing risk management

While the strategy is active, it is necessary to continually evaluate its performance and eventually modify the capital allocated to that trading system in order to regularize the equity line, as we have seen before.

This translates then into the modification of the allocated risk and of the parameters of the trading system itself, for example the stop loss, the take profit and the distribution of entries and exits.

To manage the risk on the trading system, we have 2 methods:

- **Fixed risk**

This method is good for high frequency speculative trades and allows us to predetermine the risk for each position.

For example, if the position goes to stop loss, the setup will be triggered and we will lose R (capital at risk).

The R value will need to be modified over time based on the results of the trade by adjusting it.

For example, if a trade is particularly performing, we will place a higher nominal R.

In the case of a more volatile setup, however, we will lower the capital at risk R, even to the point of excluding the entire strategy if performance is poor over the long term.

- **Capital allotment**

Capital allotment is more effective on medium/long-term trades (trend followers, accumulation plans and swing trading).

In this case the trading system will only work on one lot of the allocated capital.

For example, if 100% is the capital allocated on the TS and we want to use only 10%, we can further divide this 10% in 3 lots (that is 3.333333% for every lot) and every lot will be independent from each other.

Consequently, based on the results of the trade, the size will change by itself, as opening the position with the whole lot will auto-balance the size of the trade (if we are gaining the size increases, if we are losing it decreases).

Wanting to separate the trade into multiple lots will generate trades that are independent from each other and above all self-managed, as we will use the entire lot for each opening or closing of the position.

This practice is very useful for long-term trades, because it is easier to manage them this way, rather than calculating a risk on a trade where the stop loss is not involved (e.g. a trend follower).

LOSS MANAGEMENT: MANAGING SERIES OF LOSSES

The topic of the risk is extremely useful when speaking of Loss Management or management of the series of losses, because the first objective is the regularization of the drawdown, its decrease.

The risk/capital allocated must be dynamically modified according to the results of the trading system.

Modifying in a dynamic way the risk, or capital allocated in the case of allotment, on the basis of the results of the trading system.

How?

- By avoiding "compounding losses"

In the rush to recover losses, we can fall into the temptation of risking further and thus losing even more.

A series of losses is psychologically tough, we lose also in terms of effectiveness.

Statistically, after a certain number of losses, it is easier to lose again because we make mistakes due to lack of clear-headedness.

We should ask ourselves: is the trading system losing effectiveness?

The rule is:

After N losses (where the N value is decided in the planning phase), reduce the risk by X% for each further series of Y losses.

For example, if Y=1 and N=3

After 3 losses, for each further Y loss, reduce the risk by 5%.

Or:

After 2 losses, for every 2 losses, reduce the risk by 10%.

We lose 2 times= 0

We lose 4 times= 10%

We lose 6 times= 20% ...etc.

These are all parameters that you can decide by yourself, evaluate, test, see what works best to have an equity line as smooth as possible.

The important thing is to reduce exposure as the number of losses in a series increases.

We will see this in detail in the chapter on position sizing, but in the meantime let's learn the concept and this rule.

- Capital allotment:

As far as the capital allotment is concerned, the Radios in Losses is already integrated, since the lot decreases in value in the case of a series of losses and the exposure diminishes by itself.

WIN MANAGEMENT: MANAGING SERIES OF PROFITS

On the other side of the coin, we find Win Management, i.e. the management of the series of profits, which is equally important.

Compounding Wins

In this case, Compounding Wins must be done.

After a series of profits, it is good to increase the risk.

Obviously, we must be careful about euphoria and overexposure, since a series of profits could activate the deepest part of our emotionality, we feel invincible and therefore tend to risk too much.

- Risk Comfort Zone:

There is a particularly interesting concept here, which is the Risk comfort zone: once we achieve a nice profit, we feel "justified" to risk more.

This is because we convince ourselves that even if we go into loss and the loss is greater than the nominal loss, we will still be losing something that we have already gained!

In such cases, a useful thing to do is to work in steps, following this rule:

After N profits, increase the risk by X% for each further series of Y profits, up to a maximum of Z.

That is, after a series of profits (N), after every two or three new profits (Y), for example, increase the risk by a certain percentage (X%) until you reach a maximum (Z).

Capital allotment:

- Setting a threshold, above which excess capital is deposited into another lot.
- Reinvesting the surplus capital in a new lot, protecting the capital, reducing the risk of compounding losses, amplifying operation and regularizing the equity line.

Otherwise, with the first Loss we would risk losing a good part of the profits, because in this case we operate with the whole capital.

SUSPENSION OF A TRADING SYSTEM

In case we suspect that the trading system is losing effectiveness, we can consider its suspension according to the following criteria, defined during the planning phase:

- **Average return of the last X samples in negative**

The TS can have a return lower than X%, for example, due to a series of factors:

- Sudden drop in the win rate at equal average R/R;
- Sudden drop in average R/R at equal win rate;
- Capital lot reduced to a percentage below the threshold;

(e.g., if the lot falls below 70% of the maximum capacity, we can start considering suspension).

- **Maximum drawdown of the last X samples greater than a certain threshold**
- **Excessively long series of losses**

E.g., 8/10 losses in a row.

- **Operation frequency drastically dropped**

The TS no longer opens positions and no longer generates signals.

The important thing is to have clear criteria to suspend or close a trading system, based on the achievement of certain thresholds which are negative for our operation.

LOSS ANALYSIS

Loss analysis helps us to study the causes of poor performance of a trading system that used to work well, in order to understand where it can be improved.

Let's look at some of them.

Is it necessary to modify the Stop loss placement?

If after examining our losses one by one we realize that the stop loss is often triggered unintentionally, we will need to change it.

Is it necessary to change the Take profit placement?

In case the take profit is often narrowly missed, we will need to change it.

Is it necessary to introduce a Trailing stop or Risk exclusion?

In case the results are irregular, we will consider whether to introduce the trailing stop, which follows the market, or the risk exclusion, which liquidates part of the position to exclude our risk and keep the rest open.

The latter will reduce the potential profit but regularize the drawdown.

Is it necessary to exclude some poorly performing setups?

In case we realize that it is precisely the setup that ruins the strategy, we can exclude it.

CONCLUSIONS

Before putting a trading system into production, it is essential to evaluate its performance and introduce it gradually.

Evaluating the performance before putting the TS into production is mandatory, even if you have to wait months.

On the basis of the time at your disposal and of your predispositions, estimate how many TS to keep active, and their parameters.

For example, we could keep active a TS that operates speculatively, one that has a simple accumulation plan, one that integrates both according to certain rules, one that integrates long and short with other rules...

The important thing is to know them as if they were our brothers, we must know how they work.

Always evaluate a TS also while it is in production and eventually modify it or suspend it.

It is necessary to start from one TS and then eventually increase the size of our activity "recruiting" new trading systems.

Only once the TS already existing are active and work well, we will be able to increase our activity.

If they do not perform as well as hoped, we must concentrate on them, continue to evaluate them (even while they are in production) and eventually modify or suspend them.

Adapt to market conditions, always trying out new trading systems.

Never stand still because the market is dynamic and changes.

If a trading system has always worked, we should not rely only on it because it may suddenly stop working.

Also, from the company's point of view, we must have a Research and Development department and look for new TS that adapt to the ever-changing conditions of the market.

The Trading Journal is indispensable for reporting the results of your trades and evaluating them accordingly.

All these parameters must be written down and evaluated in the Trading Journal.

THE TRADER'S JOURNAL

The Trading Journal is one of the most important things to remain profitable over time, because it allows us to constantly evaluate our positions and see where we are wrong, where we can risk more by allocating more capital and where we should reduce the allocated capital to reduce losses.

In short, thanks to it, we can make the results of our trading more regular.

Besides, it allows us to expand our horizons by recruiting new strategies where appropriate or to exclude others that perform worse than the average.

It gives us numerical data which is what we have to rely on, otherwise we continue to improvise.

In this chapter we will learn how to design a trading journal, how to fill it and maintain it over time.

DRAFTING THE TRADING JOURNAL

The Trading Journal is the diary of our trades.

It has a dual purpose: monitoring and evaluating.

Thanks to the trading journal, we can have an overview of what we are doing, of the strategy we are applying and moreover we will be able to evaluate every single operation that we make with different degrees of granularity: from the single operation to the set of operations that is part of a trading system, up to the performance of a particular asset class, a particular market condition, etc.

Granularity is very important to continue to self-evaluate, to be always active and try to adapt to the market that is in continuous evolution.

WHY A TRADING JOURNAL?

Let's return to the metaphor of the Trader who is like the entrepreneur hiring his/her Trading Systems that are his/her employees.

The trading system consists of a series of setups that obey certain rules, a strategy (e.g. the approach to the bullish market, following the test of resistances, following the bounces on trendlines, etc.).

And then there is the single setup, that is the single bounce on the moving average, therefore deciding where to enter, where to put the stop loss and where to put the take profit.

We will have to evaluate constantly, without ever stopping, every trading system.

This is a tedious and demanding operation, but very important if one wants to maintain a good performance over time.

The main purpose of the Trading Journal is to understand what is performing well and what is performing badly:

- Understanding where to allocate more or less risk capital;
- Understanding whether to exclude some or include new ones.

In a nutshell, what performs well can be pushed more and therefore more capital can be allocated in that particular setup, on that particular Trading System, on that particular market condition.

On the contrary, we can decide to allocate less capital or even to exclude certain setups, strategies or market conditions, if we see that they perform very badly and for a long period of time.

We can also exclude or include new ones, because there will also be a part dedicated to those trading systems that we have not experimented, but we could.

This will be a kind of on-the-fly test, a real-time test that we do while executing our real strategies.

It can be a test of a variation of a strategy we are using or a completely new setup that will replace the backtesting phase.

To do this, we need:

- **A standard against which to objectively evaluate our performance;**
- **A log of operations that meets the standard, making them objective, assessable and comparable.**

This log is the maximum degree of granularity we will have, the single operation, the single result.

The whole of these products will result in mass statistics that are part of the monitoring.

DEFINING THE STANDARD

The first thing to do is to define the standard:

What do we write in the Trading Journal?

How do we quantify the results?

Adapt the trade according to size and stop loss, taking nominal risk capital R as a parameter.

There are two types of trade:

High frequency trades

Performance is assessed over a large number of trades.

- Profits and losses already in relative, comparable terms;
- Good for trades with predefined risk and profit (setup);
- R/R: Risk/Reward ratio;
- Average profit and drawdown expressed as a function of R.

In this case we have seen that we consider capital at risk as a parameter. For example, starting from high frequency trades the setup will be:

- Breakout retest, we enter at the retest of Resistance.
- We place the stop loss at the Spike just below the resistance, which has become support with the Flip, and on the hourly candles.
- We place the take profit at the first resistance zone, which is above the one we broke.

We will repeat this setup N times and will therefore have:

- A nominal risk capital of our choice (which we will open or close and then modify based on performance).
- Profits and losses in relative terms, so we will have a take profit in the first resistance zone above the Breakout.
- In function of the capital at risk and the parameter of stop loss (that, as I have said, will be under the spike and we will see how much the zone of Take profit is wide), we define a risk/return relationship.

So, if we go to stop loss we lose R, and this is the parameter we have decided, while if we go to take profit we gain XR, which can be 2R, 3R, etc.

It all depends on the risk/return.

Once we have 50-100 such samples, we will take an average and see how it went over time (average R/R, average R, average profit, average or maximum drawdown, etc.) to assess its regularity (the more predictable the better) and obviously the mere profit.

Follower trades

Far fewer positions are opened, but the effectiveness of these Trend-based positions is important.

They are systems that have less chance of success and often fail, but when they ride the trend they can be very profitable.

They will be trades without a predefined stop loss, so we will evaluate the operations according to the percentage of capital employed because we cannot define the capital at risk.

- Lot-related profit and loss

Evaluating entry and exit signals, overall profit over time, series of losses.

- Unknown R/R

We will have a much simpler evaluation, with fewer parameters, a lower frequency of operations, a capital employed (a loss and a gain) on it in percentage, unknown risk-return, so we simply rely on the Trend.

In conclusion we will scale the capital employed according to possible performance and the strategy itself.

EVALUATION DATA

We have understood how to write down positions and now we need to understand how to evaluate them according to the standard.

Write down as much information as possible at each opening and closing of position.

- Strategy and setup on which we operated.

Assuming to have both follower and high frequency trades that coexist, we must note the TS to which the position belongs (e.g., strategy: breakout retest, setup: breakout downrange...).

- Bias on different time frames, analyzing the trend.

Understanding the market situation in which we opened the position for evaluative and statistical purposes (Is the market bullish or bearish? Monthly or daily?).

- Our emotional situation (the most difficult part to evaluate).

In this case, we could give ourselves a score from +5 to -5 on positivity and confidence towards a trade. For example: what are we thinking as we open the position?

Cumulative data

Finally, all this collected data, this granularity is used to make averages, higher level observations.

Then we will make cumulative data for each trading system, for each setup, for each market condition, etc...

They are statistical analyses aimed at monitoring the trend and especially if there are correlations or dependencies between one parameter and another.

For example, do we see that our strategies work better when the market is Bullish?

We will take advantage of the consequences and deliver more risk when the market is Bullish during that strategy.

For this reason, we will pay attention to R/R, maximum or average Drawdown, maximum or average Win Rate, etc.

Portfolio overview

Understanding the capital allocation on the different trading systems and assets (as we have seen in the risk pyramidization).

Equity line:

Maintaining a regular equity line by "diluting" the profit earned on high-risk assets and moving it to lower risk assets.

ADDITIONS TO THE TRADING JOURNAL

- **Write down, separately, also the trades not executed, with appropriate reasons and simulating the results.**

In this way you will have the opportunity to integrate new TS into trading.

- **Consider appropriate inclusive moves.**
- **In order to improve your operation, write down hypothetical variations of a setup or real trade (different SL/TP, etc.).**

For example, if you have a strategy that often goes to stop loss and then the Trade goes as expected, remaining faithful to the strategy, write down a hypothetical variation (perhaps widening a little the stop loss).

Once obtained a certain number of samples, evaluate whether to apply the variation or not.

- **Take into account the different psychology of a simulated trade.**

Avoid the overexposure from simulated trading.

- **Write down a series of corrective operations executed in the strategy (ins/outs of different TS, capital reallocations, modification and exposure, etc.).**

THE VALUE OF EMPIRICAL DATA

The data from the Trading Journal allows us to monitor objectively the performance of our trading systems.

The empirical data that we are building is what is most valuable in Trading because there is no such thing as absolute data, what works best for us will not work for someone else because everyone has their own personal approach to the market and to trading.

Trading is one of the most personal things that exist and therefore there is nothing more useful than keeping a diary of this kind.

Constructing it autonomously pushes us towards self-knowledge and towards the correct trading mindset.

Defining a threshold value

By looking backwards at a trade system, we can see when it was performing and when it was not. By doing so, we can define threshold values beyond which to exclude or include new trading systems.

CONCLUSIONS

- The Trading Journal is fundamental;
- It is the only way to have everything under control;
- It avoids last-minute emotional modifications;
- The TJ must be built according to your needs;
- It needs great dedication: maintaining, historicizing and modifying over time.

POSITION SIZING

In this chapter we will deal with Position Sizing, which allows us to optimize all trade parameters and keep everything under control.

Apply statistics and probability to your setups to find the optimal size and risk.

Position sizing is the discipline that studies how to vary the size, the optimal risk capital of each position and aims to obtain it through statistical calculations that take into account various factors.

These factors can be the riskiness of a position, how often it goes to stop loss, how often it goes to take profit, what its average results are, etc.

In this last part we will see a statistical approach, with some mathematical formulas, to find these parameters, how to calculate how much capital to put in a specific position and above all why.

THE IMPORTANCE OF POSITION SIZING

Let's start by understanding why it is important to do position sizing and not open positions with a random or fixed size.

The position should be sized according to the characteristics of the specific setup, in particular:

- Probability of success or probability of profit;
- R/R ratio, what we would lose.

The purpose of position sizing should be to allocate more capital when the probability is higher and less when it is lower.

It is a very simple concept: the Trader does not keep operating all the time.

The traders who are most successful in the long run are the ones who stand still most of the time and when they see high-profitability, high-probability setups they load on them a lot, not afraid to raise the risk when it's the right time.

Probability and R/R are usually inversely correlated.

The probability of success of a position and the risk/reward ratio are often inversely correlated.

Usually, when there is a very high-risk reward, the win rate tends to fall, even well below 50%, and vice versa.

Sometimes the market shows inefficiencies: P and R/R both high.

They are extremely difficult to find: you have to go and experiment with setups in particular conditions, you have to be an expert to do so.

Finding these inefficiencies means having both the probability of success and a high and profitable risk/return over time.

If you find them, you can increase the size because it will be worth it.

In short, if you find a setup to exploit you should hold it and load on it more, but if a setup is mediocre you will load less.

The important thing, of course, is to have an overall situation of profit.

PROBABILITY AND RISK/RETURN

Let's go a little deeper into the concepts of probability and risk/return.

Probability: inverse of position risk

- Estimated with the win rate of the trading journal:

It can be calculated with the percentage of setups that have gone into profit.

For example, if a setup has a 50% win rate, it means that statistically one in two times it goes to take profit and one to stop loss.

What does it mean that probability is the inverse of position risk?

A low win rate corresponds to a high position risk.

- Each setup and condition will have its own probability:

They are independent, and each will have its own probability and average risk and return.

They can then be ranked on different market conditions (bullish, bearish, ranging, on different assets, etc.).

- More samples = more consistent estimate:

In short, more detail means more chances to go and find that situation where we have both a high risk/return and a high win rate.

- Need to find an average value:

We should at least give ourselves a minimum threshold of samples below which we consider the statistic inconsistent.

We can also calculate the variation on those results or the standard deviation, to understand even better the consistency of the results.

Risk/Return: it depends on the chart

- R/R calculation with the visual aid of technical analysis which serves to understand the risks and the potential of a position.

- It is quantified using reasonable stop losses and take profits.
- FTA: first significant resistance/support on the time frame.

The First Trouble Area is a more than reasonable estimate on which we can close the position. It is, in fact, the first significant resistance/support on the same time frame on which we opened the position.

THE KELLY CRITERION

Let's go into a little more detail and try to use the following formula.

$$f^* = \frac{bp - q}{b} = \frac{p(b + 1) - 1}{b}$$

The simplest approach to a probabilistic financial problem

This formula is very simple as far as position sizing is concerned and I have reported it because I consider it an optimal example to use.

It's called the Kelly criterion and it's an extremely simple approach to a probabilistic financial problem: how much should we bet if we know the odds of winning?

What is at stake?

Values:

F^*= % of optimal capital to be used (capital at risk R)

b= profit in case of winning (R/R)

p= probability of winning (Wine rate)

q= probability of loss (=1-p)

Example:

Setup with Win Rate = 30% and R/R = 3

F^*= (0.3*(3+1)-1)/3= 0.067 → 6.7% is the optimal capital at risk according to Kelly.

So, we can follow Kelly for a simplified approach, unless we have special needs...

BEYOND THE KELLY CRITERION

Let's take a step forward and introduce the so-called dynamic Risk Management.

Risk management is closely related to position sizing because we manage the overall risk of our portfolio by varying the position sizing according to certain conditions, especially when we are in a condition of series of wins or losses.

The Kelly criterion model does not include the dynamic components of Risk management.

- Management of series of wins:

A buffer is created to mitigate a possible subsequent loss and we can risk a little more.

- Management of series of losses:

There may be an anomaly in the setup or something not calculated.

In these cases, it is better to mitigate the size of the position until tending to zero, if necessary, to avoid exaggerated drawdowns.

How to adjust capital at risk R

There are two types of adjustment:

- Linear adjustment:

It consists in increasing or decreasing each subsequent loss/gain by a certain amount.

Example: Size = R = 1

After 3 wins, R will become 1.1, then 1.2, then 1.3 and so on.

- Exponential adjustment:

Increase by a percentage for each loss/gain after a certain amount.
Example:

After 3 wins, 10% increase in R.

R=1 after 3 wins will be R 1.1, then 1.21, with an exponential increase.

Let's take a look at some concrete examples both on the compounding wins (increasing the size after a series of wins) and on the cutting losses (decreasing the size after a series of losses).

COMPOUNDING WINS

Compounding Wins

- For each win after the third, we increase the risk by 0.5R (Linear compounding).

Win1, Win2, Win3= R(+3R)
   W4=1.5R L4=-1.5R
   W5=2R L5=-2R

So, after the first 3 wins (W), at the fourth win the size will increase to 1.5R (note the increase in the chart).

Clearly, in case of loss, we lose -1.5R, losing 0.5 of the previous win.

This may be okay because we have our "buffer" (which is the 3R) that we just gained from the series of 3 wins.

The more compounding comes into play, the more impact the first loss has on our result.

- First loss = sizing again R

At the first loss, we can choose between resetting the sizing and restarting from R or decreasing it by the same amount as the compounding (or by its double or half depending on our needs).

At the end we make a scheme that can help us to understand how to manage the various parameters according to the position that we are managing.

- Exponential compounding = +/-X%

It tends to increase or decrease more or less X% at each step.

CUTTING LOSSES

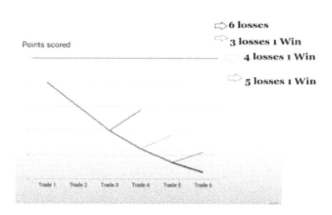

- At each loss after the third, we decrease the risk by 25% R.

L1, L2, L3 = -3R

L4 = 0.75R

L5 = 0.56R

The first three losses give use -3R overall, at the fourth loss we make a 25% cut which gives us a result of -0.75R (note the slope of the curve in the chart).

With the fifth loss, there will be a 25% reduction, so it becomes -0.56R.

On the contrary, if we make a win, we will have +0.75R and we won't completely recover the previous loss, but it's a situation where we give more weight to mitigating the loss risk rather than recovering it.

It is more important to reduce the risk of a higher drawdown than to be in a hurry to recover the loss.

- At each win, it is better to take a step back.

In the classic case of risk management of cutting losses, it's better to take a step back.

If we have a size of 0.75R, we take a step back and return to 0.50R.

Also here we will be able to decide how to regulate ourselves, whether to make a step back of R, of its double or half. The important thing is to maintain a regular Equity line and to minimize the drawdown.

PARAMETERS OF DYNAMIC RISK MANAGEMENT

So how do we keep all this under control? What do we rely on?

Modulable parameters

- Deciding whether cutting or compounding is linear or exponential;
- Defining the size of cuts or increments;
- Determining the reactivity, i.e., after how many wins or losses to intervene;
- Determining the imbalance between Compounding wins and Cutting losses (deciding whether to focus more on compounding or cutting).

The modulable parameters depend on:

- Regularity of equity line and maximum drawdown;
- If we have a lower drawdown, we can minimize cutting losses;
- If we have a low drawdown and a regular equity line, we can maximize compounding wins;
- Riskiness of the position;
- If the win rate is low and we have a high R/R, it is advisable to use low-impact risk management;
- If the win rate is high but the R/R is low, a higher risk management is needed.

(Setup low risk low reward)

Obviously, before defining any parameters, we will need to do our studies and backtests, as well as our Trading journal.

CONCLUSIONS

- It is essential to estimate the parameters of probability and potential gain in great detail (Trading Journal).
- Use the "confidence" and the "buffer" gained from a series of wins to risk a little more.
- File the loss after taking others to minimize the drawdown.
- Contextualize the strategy (e.g., is a series of losses the norm?) and apply it accordingly.

Ingram Content Group UK Ltd.
Milton Keynes UK
UKHW020650270623
424112UK00014B/512